IMAGES
of Ameri

PORT CLINTON,
THE PENINSULA,
AND THE BASS ISLANDS

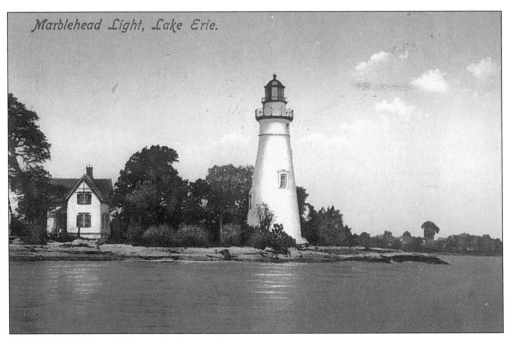

Marblehead Light, Lake Erie.

The Marblehead Lighthouse, built in 1821, is one of the best known landmarks in the area. It is pictured c.1910 with a keeper's house. The lighthouse and surrounding grounds became a state park in 1997.

IMAGES
of America

PORT CLINTON, THE PENINSULA, AND THE BASS ISLANDS

Sally Sue Witten

ARCADIA

Published by Arcadia Publishing,
an imprint of Tempus Publishing, Inc.
2 Cumberland Street
Charleston, SC 29401

Printed in Great Britain.

Library of Congress Catalog Card Number: 99-069083

For all general information contact Arcadia Publishing at:
Telephone 843-853-2070
Fax 843-853-0044
E-Mail arcadia@charleston.net

For customer service and orders:
Toll-Free 1-888-313-BOOK

Visit us on the internet at http://www.arcadiaimages.com

CONTENTS

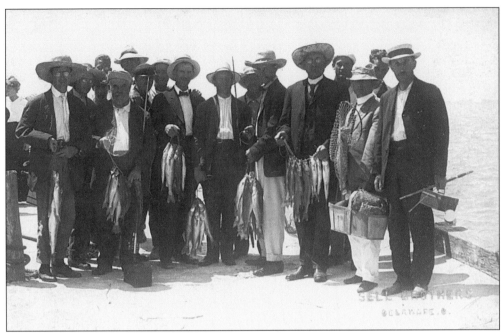

Many people are drawn to the area because of the good sport fishing. These men who got off a boat at Lakeside were pleased to display their catch c.1906.

Acknowledgments

Special thanks to Neil Allen of the Lakeside Heritage Society Museum and to Ed Isaly of the Erie Islands Historical Museum for the loan of pictures from the archives of those museums. Thanks also to the Lake County (IL) Museum/Curt Teich Postcard Archives for permission to copy Curt Teich postcards. Appreciation is expressed to several individuals who loaned pictures, including Kamille Allen, Joseph Demshok, Robert Meyers, Anne Carroll Hitchcock, Josephine Monak, Earl Wiseman, and Ruth E. Ellis. Special gratitude is due Phyllis Cermak for production assistance.

INTRODUCTION

"Walleye Capital of the World," "Northcoast Vacationland," "Chautauqua on Lake Erie," and "Put an Island in your Life" are some of the slogans used to attract tourists to Lake Erie communities in Ottawa County, Ohio. Located 75 miles west of Cleveland and 50 miles east of Toledo, Port Clinton (population 7,106) is the only actual city in the county. Pictures that follow depict the area from approximately 1880 to 1980, and illustrate scenes from just six townships in Ottawa County that border Lake Erie: Carroll, Catawba Island, Danbury, Erie, Portage and Put-in-Bay. The 1990 population of these townships was 20,009, or about half the county total. With peninsulas and islands, this small area claims 107 miles of Lake Erie coastline.

Although home to Native Americans for centuries, the first permanent settlement of the area did not occur until six years after Ohio became a state in 1803. Benajah Wolcott brought his family in 1809 to settle in Danbury Township on the Marblehead Peninsula. Danbury Township and the east side of Catawba were part of the Firelands of the Western Reserve. The Marblehead Lighthouse was built in 1821 of local limestone. Quarry operations soon prospered as limestone was shipped by boat to lake ports, and an influx of laborers to work the quarries led to the incorporation of the Village of Marblehead in 1891.

Another industry originated in 1821 when gypsum was discovered on the Sandusky Bay side of the peninsula. Several small mining and plaster-making operations, some of which were consolidated in 1902 as the U.S. Gypsum Company, developed around this discovery. The Celotex Corporation had its origin in 1906 as the American Gypsum Company. Both the U.S. Gypsum Company and Celotex Corporation remain in business nearly a century later.

In 1824, Dewitt Clinton, a New York politician and father of the Erie Canal, proposed that a canal be built from the mouth of the Portage River on Lake Erie to the Ohio River at Cincinnati. This prompted some Cincinnatians to acquire acreage at the mouth of the Portage River and to have Port Clinton platted in 1828. Permanent settlers did not arrive, however, until about 1830. The canal never materialized because examination indicated insufficient water along the route to sustain a canal. Lacking harbor facilities, Port Clinton was slower to develop industrially than some other Lake Erie communities, but still managed to advance as a commercial center.

Although squatters and landowner agents temporarily lived on the Bass Islands, the first permanent settlers did not arrive until 1843. By 1858, the first grapes were planted and a wine industry was born. After the Civil War, as the American economy evolved from agricultural to industrial, the opportunity for family vacations emerged. The Bass Islands were an easily accessible vacation place because steamboats from Detroit and Toledo to Cleveland and Buffalo made stops at the islands. Interest in the American victory over the British during the War of 1812's Battle of Lake Erie heightened interest in visiting Put-in-Bay on South Bass Island. Erection of Perry's Victory and International Peace Monument enhanced Put-in Bay's popularity. It is not unusual for South and Middle Bass Islands, with a year-round population of approximately 500, to be visited during the warm months by 20,000 people per week.

Early in the Civil War, Johnson's Island was selected as the site of a United States prison for captured Confederate soldiers. It is located in Sandusky Bay less than a mile off-shore from the Marblehead Peninsula, and about three miles across the bay from Sandusky. Previously used only for modest farming, Johnson's Island soon had facilities to accommodate 2,500 prisoners. At the end of the war in 1865, some farming resumed in the area. Three decades later, short-lived attempts were made to establish a resort, and quarry operations were undertaken twice. Eventually, the island became the location of modest summer cottages and then of more substantial year-round homes after a new causeway was built to connect the island with the peninsula. A cemetery maintained by the U.S. government with 206 Confederate graves is the only visible reminder of the prison.

Lakeside, a community on the Marblehead Peninsula, was founded by Methodists in 1873 as a Christian family resort. Its religious services were soon coupled with educational, cultural, and recreational programs. The area became part of the late 19th century chautauqua movement and is one of the few chautauquas that survive into the 21st century. Lakeside's 3,000 seat auditorium, two hotels, 700 foot dock, and other program and recreational facilities draw 7,000 to 8,000 people per week during the summer months. Smaller numbers visit during winter months for meetings and conferences.

In 1906, the Ohio National Guard acquired land west of Port Clinton for a military training facility. The site was promptly named Camp Perry in honor of Oliver Hazard Perry, hero of the Battle of Lake Erie. In addition to training the Ohio National Guard, the camp has been used as a proving ground, army induction center, prison for captured Italian and German soldiers during World War II, arena for National Rifle and Pistol matches, and training center for the Ohio Highway Patrol.

With miles of waterfront, historical sites, and modest tourist facilities in the 19th century, Ottawa County's tourism was destined to expand in the 20th century. The last chapter of this book traces how accessibility by public transportation contributed to area development. Pictured in succession are modes of transportation including steamboats, railroad, trolley or electric railway, ferries, the automobile, busses, and an airline. Tourism and industrial development both benefit from the area's adjacency to key interstates and waterways.

One
PORT CLINTON

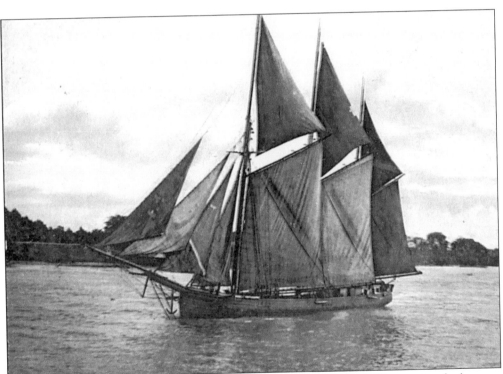

The history of Port Clinton parallels the history of boats on Lake Erie. Three-masted schooners like the one pictured here were tied up at Port Clinton into the early years of the 20th century. Some were pleasure boats for the wealthy, others utilitarian vessels that carried passengers and freight to the islands or docks in the area.

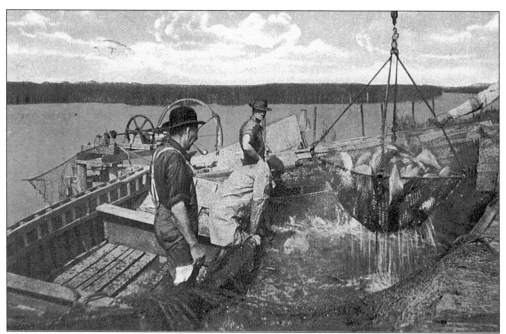

Long before it was known as "Walleye Capital of the World," Port Clinton had a thriving commercial fishing industry. The catch was clearly good in this 1920s picture. Currently, about 100,000 fishing licenses are sold annually in Ottawa County to sports fishermen.

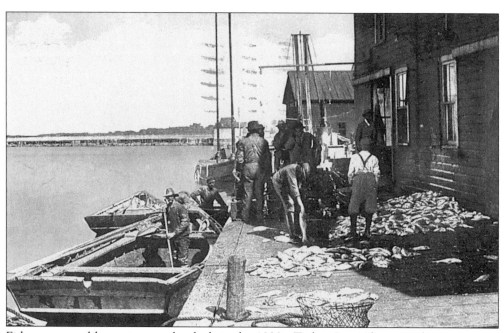

Fish were sorted by variety on the dock in the 1920s. Today, Port Clinton Fisheries Inc. not only sells locally, but also transports fish twice a week during spring and fall months to New York's Fulton Fish Market and other eastern sales outlets.

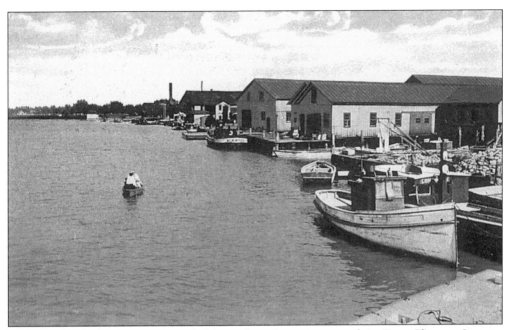

Early in the 20th century, several fish packing houses operated in Port Clinton. Ice was harvested from the lake in the winter and stored for use in shipping fish by boat or rail. Some fish houses, however, dried fish for shipment.

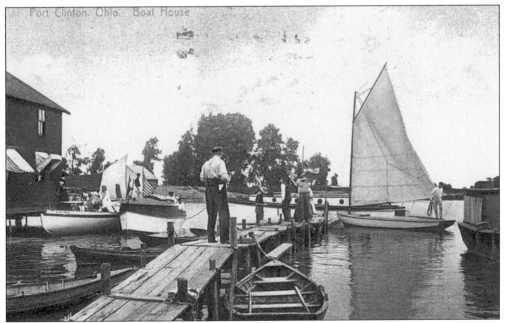

This 1906 scene shows a dock for recreational boaters and a boat house on the left. In 1997, there were 121 marinas in Ottawa County with docks for 15,875 boats. This represented 36% of all marinas in Ohio.

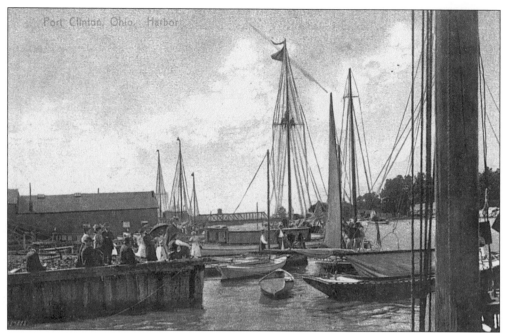

In 1911, spectators gathered to wait for a sailboat race to begin. The old bridge across the Portage River is seen in the background.

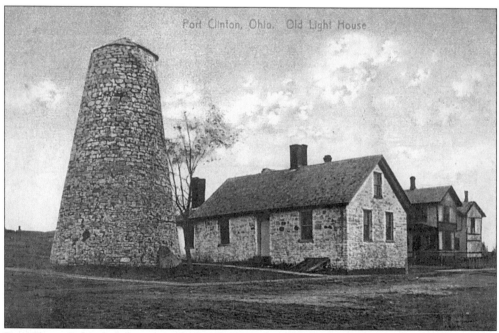

Port Clinton's first lighthouse was built in 1833 with an adjacent keeper's house at the corner of Perry Street and Adams (formerly Market Street). The lighthouse was not used between 1870 and 1899, the year it was finally torn down. Currently, the Garden at the Lighthouse Restaurant is close to this location.

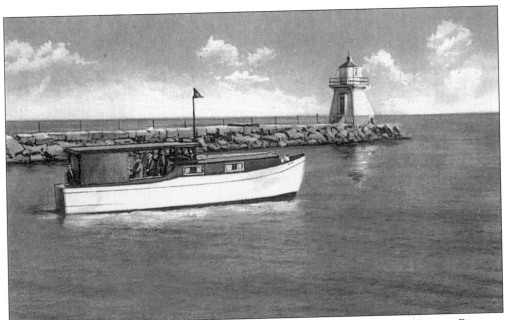

In 1896, a second lighthouse was built on the breakwater at the mouth of the Portage River, as shown in this 1930s picture. Eventually replaced by a light on a steel frame, this lighthouse was moved as a curiosity to what is now Brand's Marina. The building in which kerosene was stored to fuel the light is in Waterworks Park, and now used for storage of sports equipment.

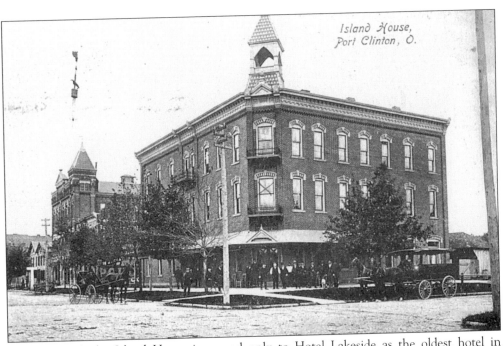

Island House, Port Clinton, O.

Built in 1886, the Island House is second only to Hotel Lakeside as the oldest hotel in continuous operation in Ottawa County. Notice the horse-drawn vehicle used for public transportation at lower right.

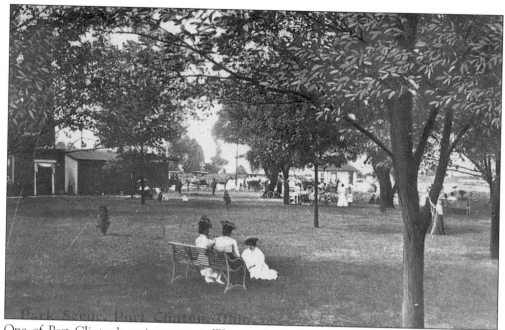

One of Port Clinton's major assets is Waterworks Park on the lakefront. It was a popular gathering place during horse and buggy days.

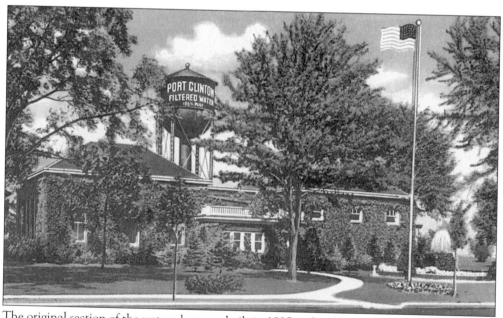

The original section of the water plant was built in 1895 with a filtration system added in 1911. The elevated tank was added in 1938 just before this picture was taken. A new water system in 1999 made this plant obsolete.

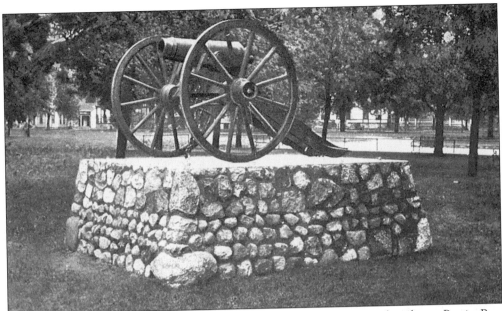

Around 1900, a British cannon, presumably from the War of 1812, was found near Put-in-Bay. It was brought to Port Clinton and mounted on a wheeled gun carriage inappropriate for a naval gun. Later more suitably mounted, it can be seen near Perry Street in Waterworks Park.

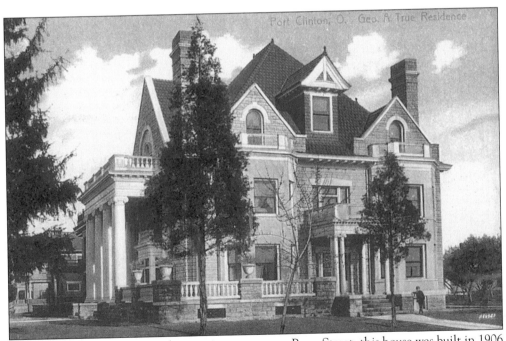

Viewed from Fulton Street with its main entrance on Perry Street, this house was built in 1906 by George A. True (1865-1931). Attorney True, an officer with the German American Bank, the Light and Power Company, and the Board of Education, was one of several generations of his family to become Port Clinton leaders.

15

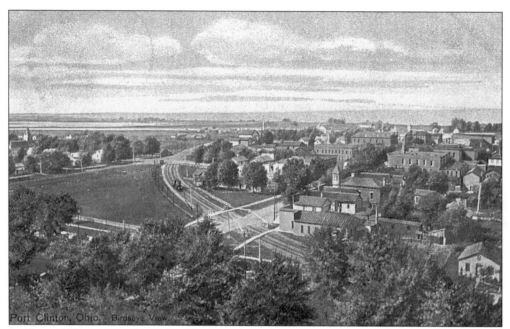

In this *c.*1901 image, the Lake Shore and Michigan Southern Railroad tracks are shown entering Port Clinton. The village population was then about 3,000. It was not until 1928, after the New York Central acquired the railroad, that overpasses were built so the tracks could be elevated.

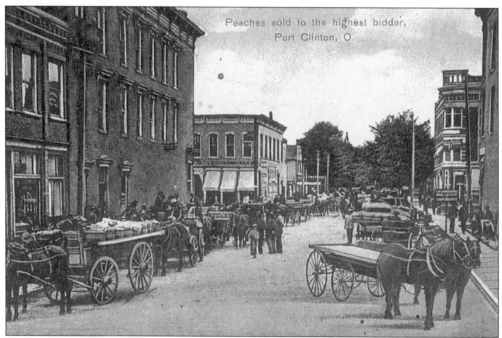

In this *c.*1906 scene, peach wagons appear on Second Street near Madison. The three-story building on the left is the Jacobs and Payne Block, completed in 1874. Altered in appearance, the building is currently occupied by Key Bank. The structure with awnings, built in 1872, is the Steidle and Detlef Block, which has always been occupied by a drug store.

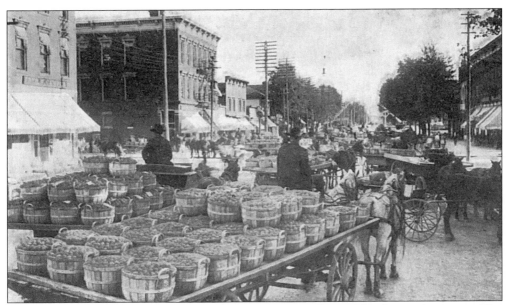

Shown here, peach wagons wait on Madison to turn onto Second for the peach auction. The railroad arms in the distance date the picture before 1928, when the overpass was built. Both a basket factory and cannery were once Port Clinton businesses.

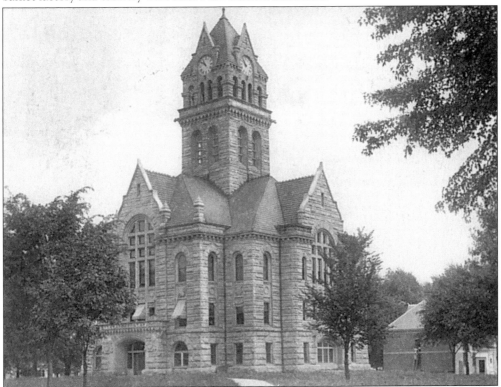

The Ottawa County Court House was built in 1900 to replace an earlier one at the same location. The jail occupied the building at the right. Interesting murals depicting Ottawa County history were later painted on the walls of one court house corridor.

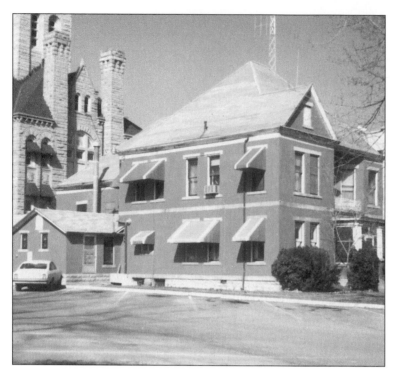

In the 1980s, a new wing was added to the court house to accommodate the sheriff's office and jail. This 1983 picture shows the old sheriff's office and jail not long before it was demolished.

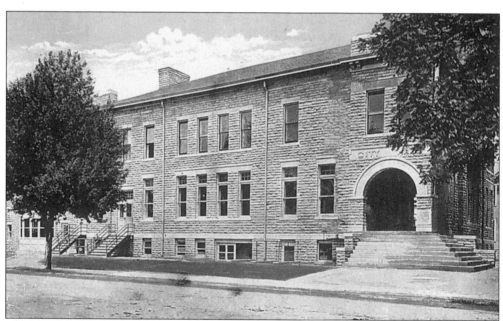

Municipal offices occupied City Hall at Second and Adams Streets from 1911 to the 1990s, when they were moved to handicapped-accessible facilities. From 1913 to 1930, some space was used in City Hall for the first library and later for the Ottawa County Museum. The future of this building has not been determined.

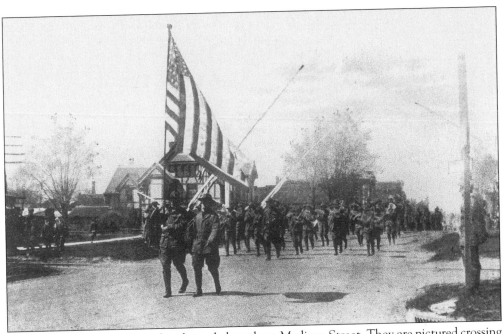

Around 1917, the Boy Scout band paraded south on Madison Street. They are pictured crossing railroad tracks where the viaduct was later built.

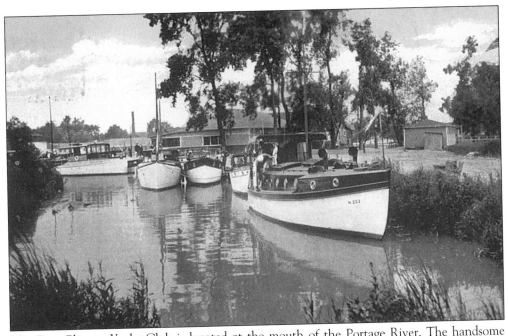

The Port Clinton Yacht Club is located at the mouth of the Portage River. The handsome wood boats of the era are shown in this 1931 picture. Dock space has been greatly expanded in recent years.

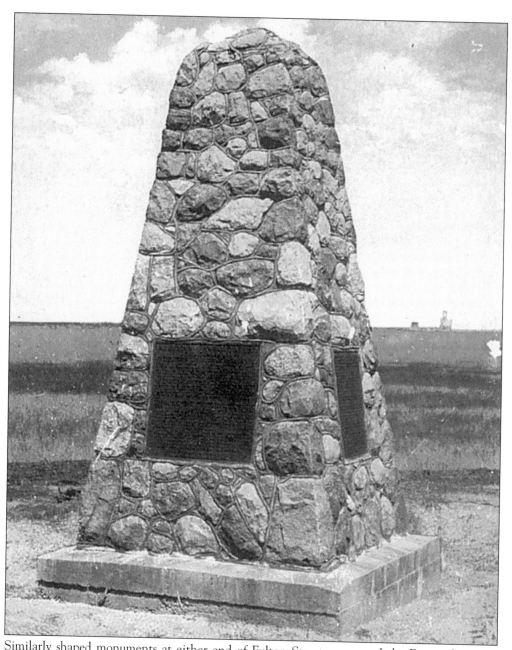

Similarly shaped monuments at either end of Fulton Street—one on Lake Erie and one on Sandusky Bay—recall early history. The one on the bay marks the beginning of a portage across the peninsula used by Native Americans and French explorers to avoid paddling around the end of the peninsula. The one on the lake marks the end of the Scioto Trail used by Native Americans coming from southern Ohio. It was also used during the War of 1812 by troops led by General William Henry Harrison. Here, they boarded boats to reach Canada where the British were defeated on Canadian soil. The portage is called DeLery Portage because Joseph DeLery, a French explorer, described its use in his journal in 1754. Some years earlier, French explorers had built a fortification near the monument on the bay called Fort Sandoski, which was in ruins when DeLery described it in his journal.

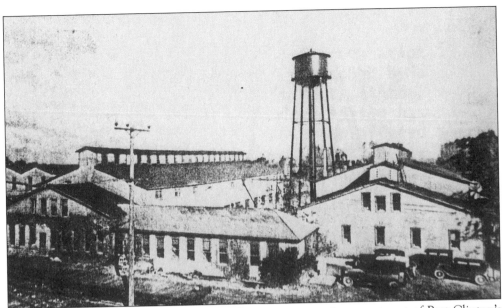

Pictured in the 1920s, the Matthews Boat Company was an important part of Port Clinton's economy from 1906 to 1974. While its boats were primarily pleasure craft, the company produced submarine chasers during World War I and patrol boats during World War II.

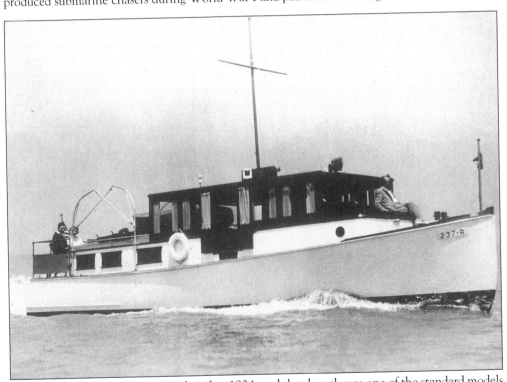

The 38-foot day cruiser was introduced in 1924, and that length was one of the standard models for many years. Custom models as long as 120 feet were built for wealthy yachtsmen. Matthews' boats were built of beautiful woods until the last few years of the company's existence, when fiberglass was substituted.

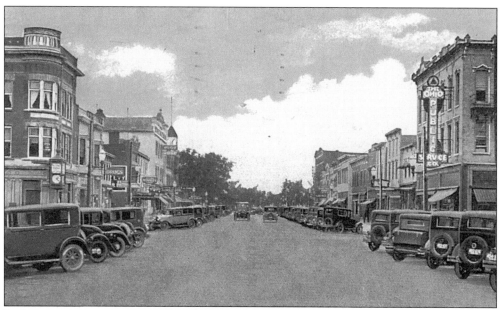

Parking space was at a premium in this 1930s picture looking north on Madison from Second Street. The building on the left with the clock, erected in 1896 by W.O. McMahan, featured a jewelry store on the first floor, and Dr. Henry Pool's first hospital on the third.

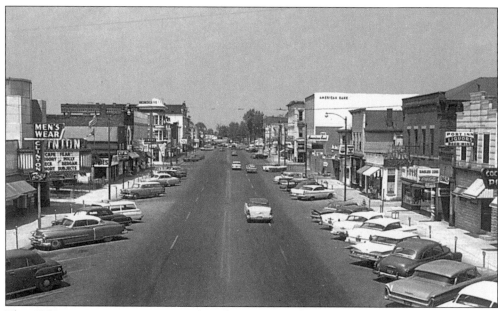

This 1970s picture presents a view of Madison Street taken from the viaduct at Third Street. False fronts had been added to a number of the old buildings including the American Bank, and the Clinton Theater was showing a Humphrey Bogart movie.

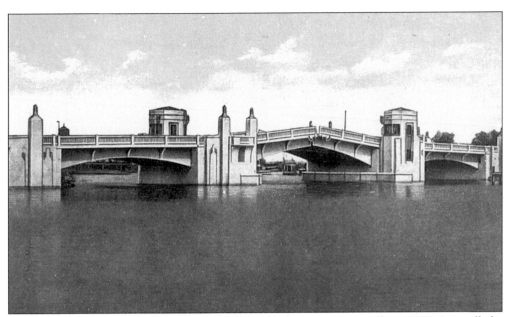

Designed in art deco style, the new Portage River Bridge opened to traffic in 1933. It is called a "double bascule" bridge because both sides are raised to allow boats to sail underneath. It was also called the "whistling bridge" because steel plate flooring gave a whistling sound when cars drove over it.

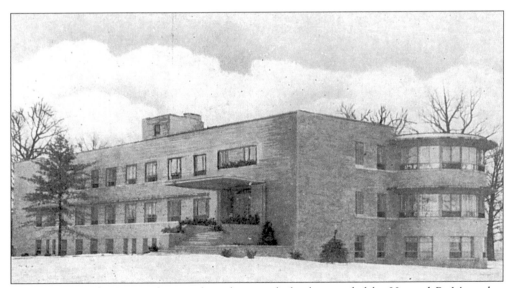

In 1940, Magruder Hospital opened its doors with funds provided by Howard B. Magruder. Located where the fairgrounds had previously been, the hospital originally had 36 beds. Several additions have more than tripled capacity and provided space for modern medical equipment.

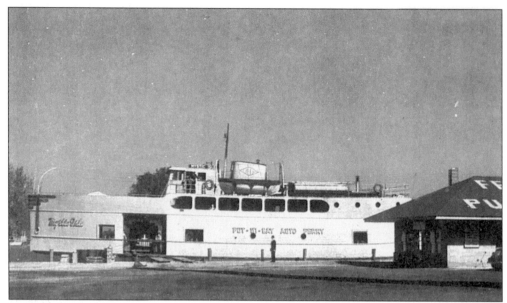

In 1947, Port Clinton leased dock space at the end of Jefferson Street to the Erie Isle Ferry Company. *The Mystic Isle* had the first auto ferry service from Port Clinton to Put-in-Bay. Successor lessees for dock space have been Parker Boat Line and now the Put-in-Bay Boat Line, which operates the *Jet Express*.

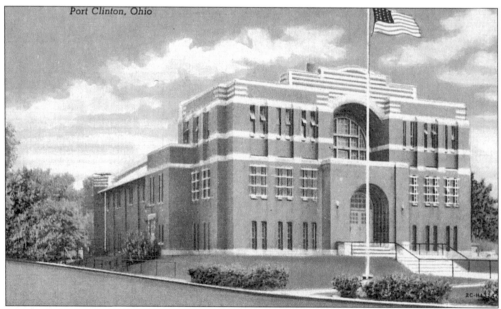

In a park behind the Armory is a memorial honoring the 22 men of the Port Clinton Tank Company who lost their lives during World War II in the Philippines. They died in combat or during the Bataan Death March. A tank is in the park as well as a memorial to other veterans. The Armory has been privately owned since soon after World War II.

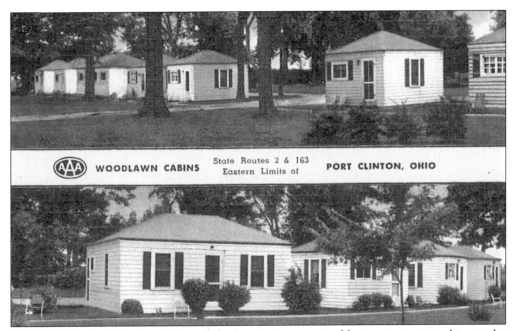

In the 1950s, the American Automobile Association gave its blessing to tourist cabins at the eastern edge of town. The wooded area with a sandy beach is now the site of a service station with nearby motels, restaurants, and condominiums.

Every few years, some Port Clinton streets are flooded due to heavy rain coupled with a strong northeaster that raises the lake level. A flooded Second Street is pictured in 1974 as viewed from Monroe Street looking east. The Tadsen Agency sign appears on the left, and the *News Herald* building on the right.

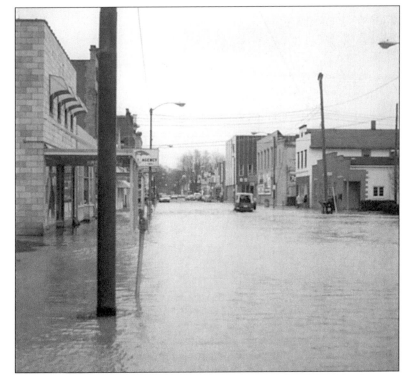

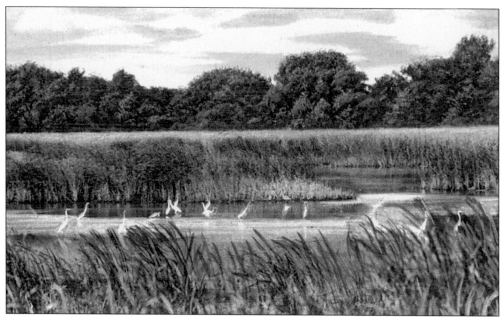

A major flyway for migrating birds, this area has witnessed more than 300 species, including the white herons of this marsh area. West of Port Clinton, state and federal governments have established wildlife preservation areas such as Magee Marsh State Reservation, Toussaint Creek Wildlife Area, and Ottawa National Wildlife Refuge.

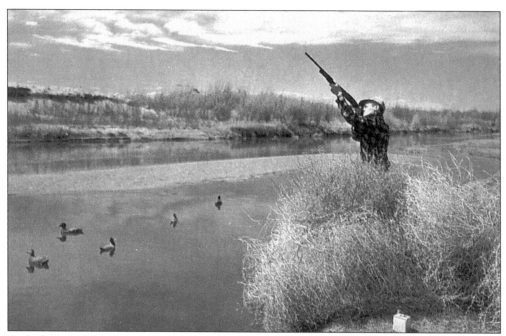

Both duck and deer hunting are popular sports in the area. Wildlife preservation authorities maintain limits via an annual lottery that selects names of those permitted to hunt.

Two

CAMP PERRY

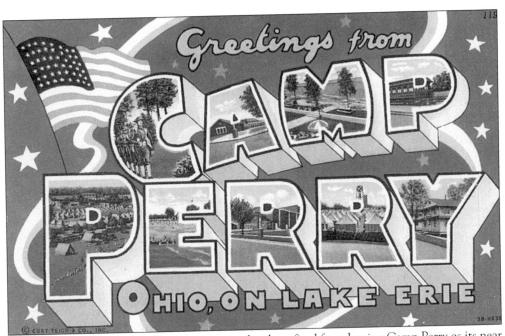

For nearly a century, Port Clinton's economy has benefited from having Camp Perry as its near neighbor. While Camp Perry serves a serious military purpose, it is also a tourist destination for families of guardsmen-in-training, or those accompanying participants to National Rifle and Pistol Matches.

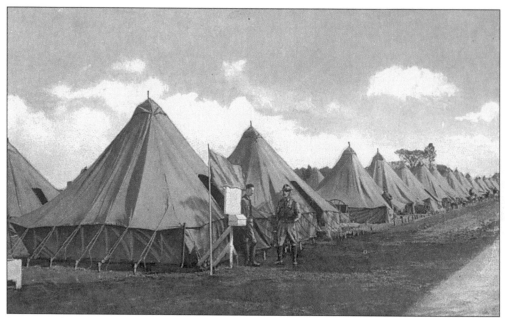

In 1906, the Ohio National Guard purchased land west of Port Clinton for training citizen soldiers. Troops initially were housed in tents like those pictured here. In the intervening years, tens of thousands of troops have trained at Camp Perry and equal numbers have participated in the annual National Rifle and Pistol Matches.

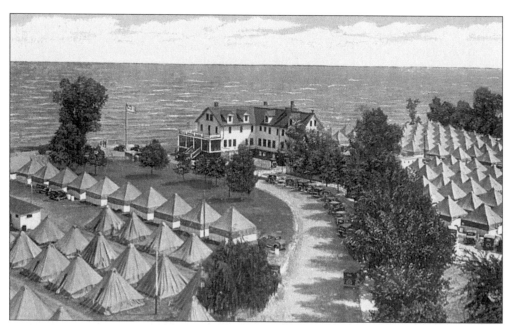

A club house adjacent to a beach area was erected in 1907, and replaced by a more modern structure 90 years later. Wives who accompanied men to National Rifle and Pistol Matches were housed in some of the nearby tents called the "squaw camp." The tents were eventually replaced by motel-like buildings.

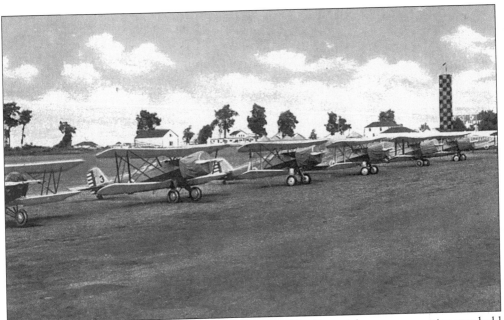

The airfield was dedicated in 1934. Prior to World War II, aerial gunnery practice was held using planes at this field.

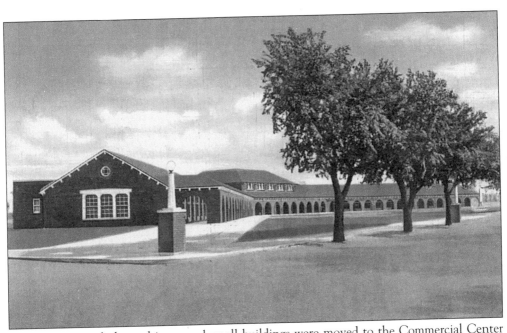

Services previously housed in several small buildings were moved to the Commercial Center upon its construction in 1936. These included the post exchange, YMCA, post office, and telephone exchange.

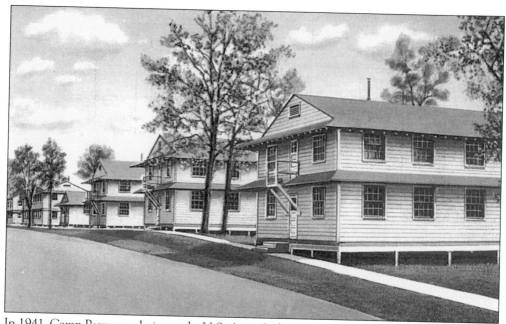

In 1941, Camp Perry was designated a U.S. Army Induction Center. Twenty-two barracks were built so that 1,000 draftees could be processed every three days.

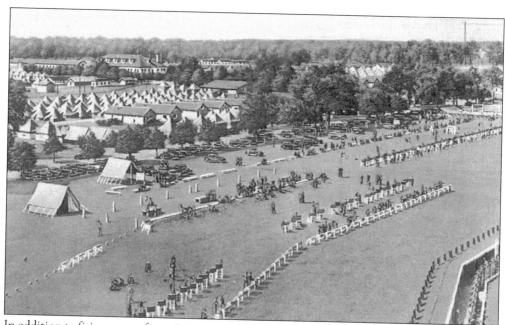

In addition to firing ranges for training purposes, Camp Perry had a prisoner of war camp during World War II. From 1943 to 1945, both Italian and German prisoners were held here. At the war's end, there were 2,000 Germans to be sent home

Three
CATAWBA ISLAND

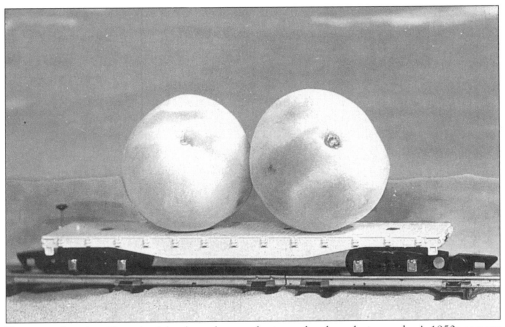

For many decades, Catawba Island was known for its orchards and vineyards. A 1950s camera buff used a bit of clever photography to illustrate Catawba's large, succulent peaches.

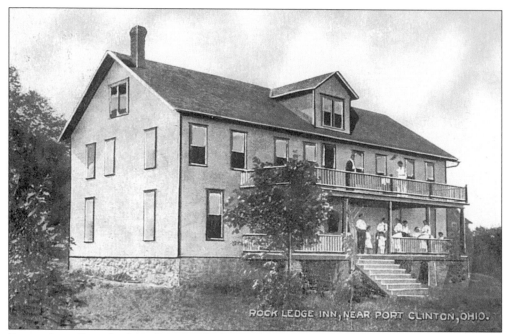

Even when Catawba Island primarily featured orchards, vineyards, and other agricultural products, vacationers were drawn to its shores. At the beginning of the 20th century, Rock Ledge Inn offered overnight tourist accommodations.

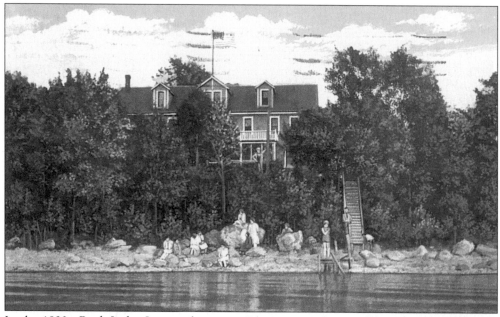

In the 1930s, Rock Ledge Inn was known as "the vacation home of the King's Daughters of Ohio," a reference to the young women who enjoyed swimming on its rocky shore. Rock Ledge Inn, with extensive renovation and cottages added, still offers accommodations for vacationers today.

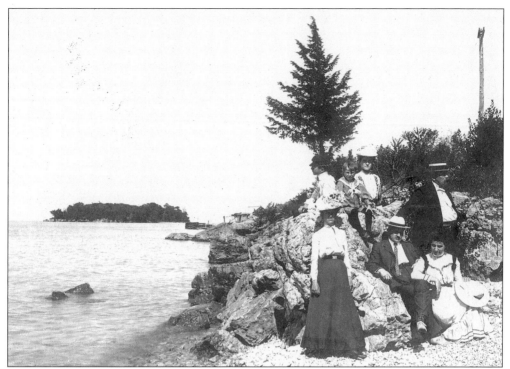

This 1906 photograph, with its Mouse Island backdrop, shows people posed near Catawba Point. President Rutherford B. Hayes had purchased the island as a retreat while he was Governor of Ohio (1876-1877). His family used the island well into the 20th century.

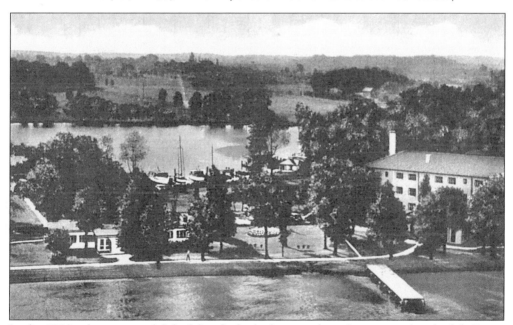

In the 1930s, this private club had few docks for boats and was known as a beach club. Later, with a name change to Catawba Island Club, its golf course and dockage for boats eclipsed the beach.

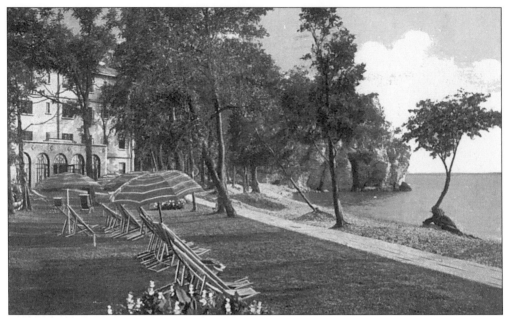

Brightly colored canvas chairs and umbrellas were the style during beach club days, though the rocky shore made for a somewhat undesirable beach.

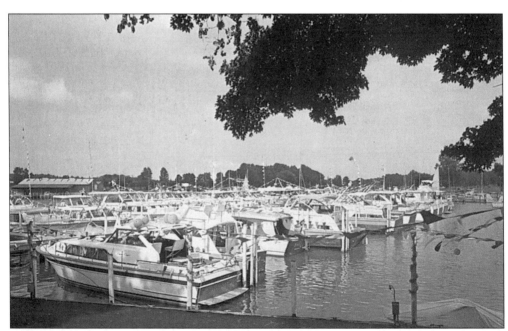

By the 1970s, the Beach Club had become the Catawba Island Club. More docks had been built in the yacht basin, and boating and playing golf on the club's course had become the big attractions.

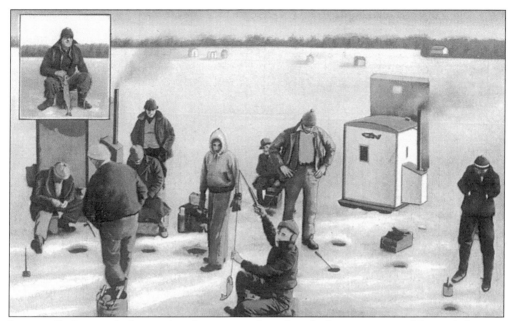

It is usually January before ice has frozen enough inches thick to permit ice fishing. A favorite ice fishing location is off shore from Catawba Island State Park.

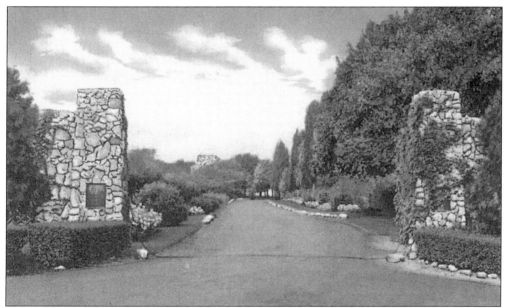

Catawba Cliffs was one of the early residential subdivisions of the area. Its beautiful homes rest on high cliffs overlooking the lake. A gate, added to the entrance several years after construction, was designed to keep out the curious.

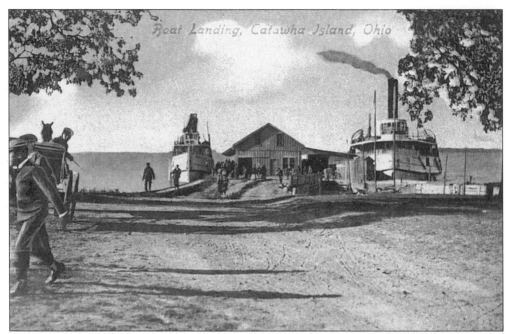

Peaches were shipped by boat in the heyday of orchards on Catawba. The *Falcon*, the small boat featured here, ran from Port Clinton. The larger boat, the *Frank E. Kirby*, ran from Detroit, and was known to load up to 5,000 bushels of peaches per trip.

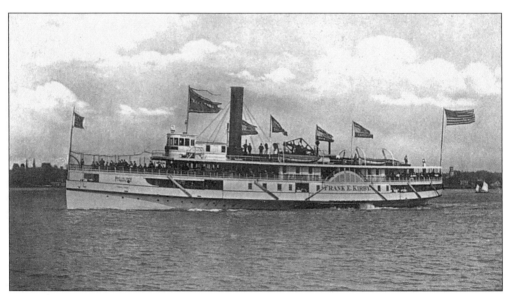

Built of steel in 1890, the *Kirby* was named for the marine architect who designed her. She was the first steamer to have electric lights. In appreciation for their business, orchard owners were given a free trip to Detroit at the end of peach season.

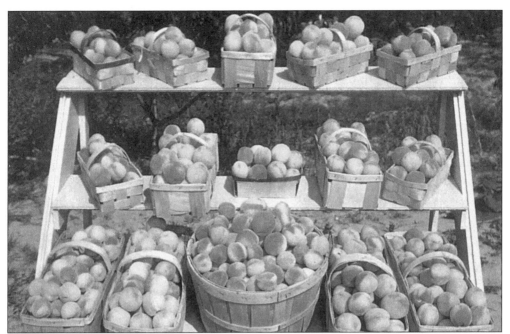

By mid-century, housing subdivisions and mobile home parks had resulted in a decline in acreage devoted to orchards, vineyards, and other agriculture. Peach crops became so small that sales could be accommodated by roadside stands. With increasing construction of homes and condominiums, even the roadside stands are disappearing today.

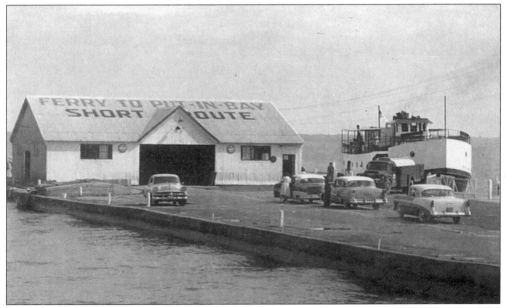

In 1945, the *South Shore* was the Miller Boat Line's first ferry built to carry autos from Catawba Point to Put-in-Bay. Note the tanker truck waiting to load, preventing islanders from being dependent on gasoline shipped in barrels.

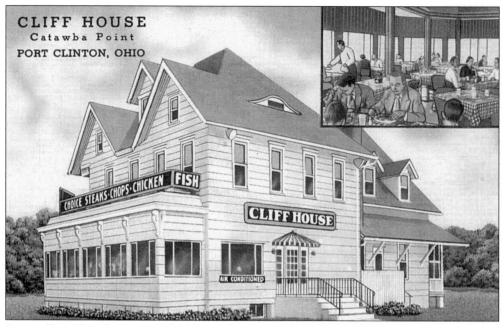

Originally a saloon known as Ruh's Place, the renovated Cliff House, located at Catawba Point, was a favorite restaurant until destroyed by fire in 1967.

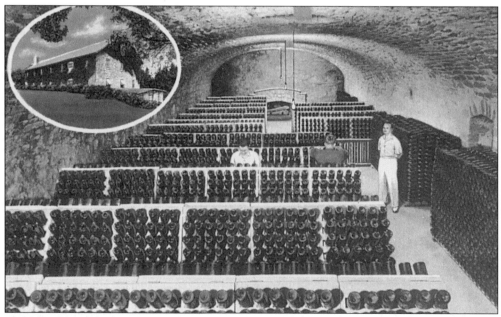

Catawba Island had such an abundance of grapes that in 1872, area growers formed a cooperative and started the Mon Ami Winery. Pictured in the 1970s, the wine cellars are housed beneath a popular restaurant. While a Mon Ami label endures, wine is no longer made on Catawba.

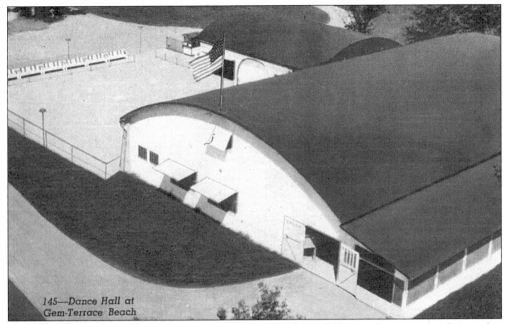

145—Dance Hall at Gem-Terrace Beach

Prior to World War I, there were several saloons and dance halls on the east side of Catawba. Post-war modernization included the Gem Terrace Beach Dance Hall, where dance marathons were held in the 1930s. The building was later converted to a roller skating rink and then to boat storage.

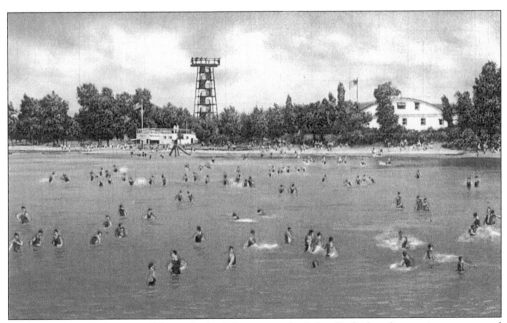

In the 1940s, swimmers could use the bath house on the left, climb the observation tower, and then go dancing at the dance hall on the right. Cottage rentals were also available.

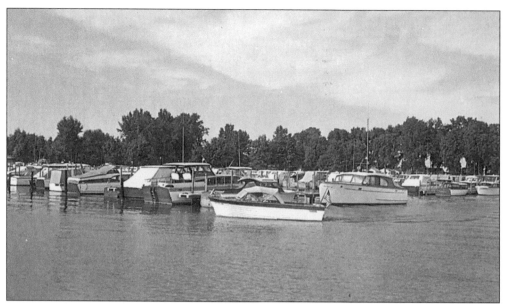

In the 1950s and 1960s, recreational boating gained popularity. Docks at Gem Boat Harbor were expanded to accommodate more boats.

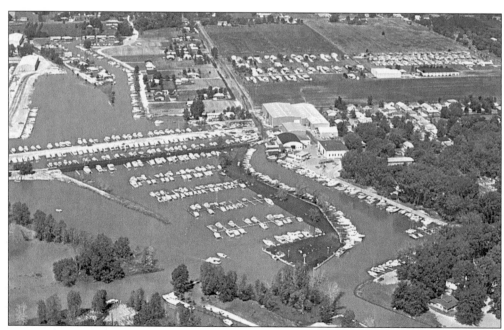

An aerial view demonstrates increased growth in recreational boating by the 1970s. Gem Boat Service offered for sale such brands of boats as Carver, Boatel, I. M. P., Lyman, Trojan, and Viking.

Four
EAST HARBOR

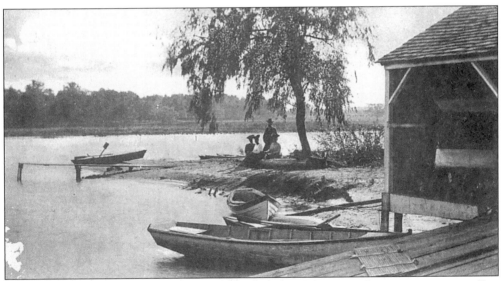

At the beginning of the 20th century, a private hunt club operated a summer resort at East Harbor known as Sandy Beach. There were facilities for swimming, picnicking, hiking, and a few very modest cottages. People could row boats from the Marblehead Peninsula to Sandy Beach, and before outboard motors, thought nothing of rowing four or five miles to a destination.

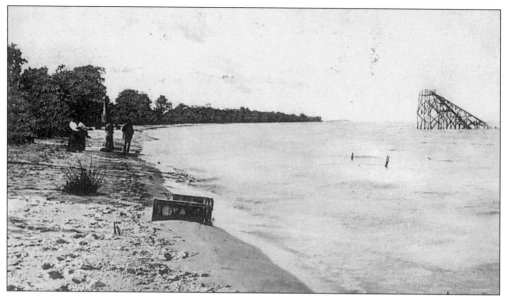

Decades before the state of Ohio built East Harbor State Park, the beach area was a privately owned resort known as Sandy Beach. Note the wonderful sliding board in this postcard from 1907.

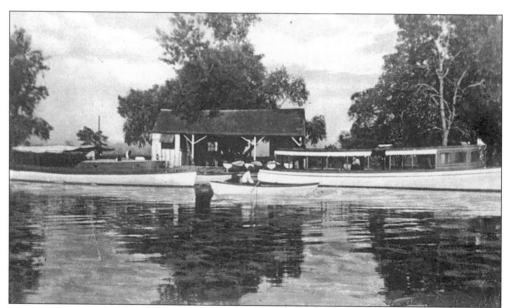

The beach area was an island accessed by boat before the State bought the property and built a causeway. Boats such as the *Summer Seas* on the left ran regularly from the Lakeside dock to Sandy Beach, and a lunch stand was located near the boat dock.

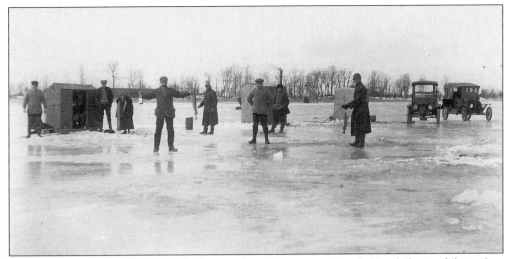

In February of 1917, the ice was thick enough to drive cars to Sandy Beach for ice fishing. Just one woman braved the cold with this group.

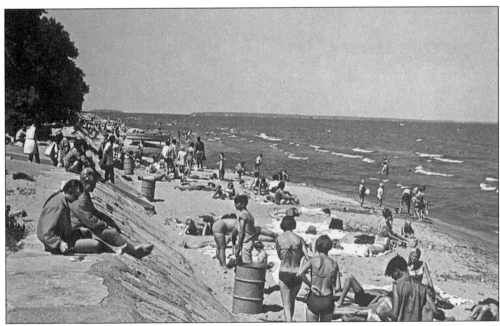

In 1945, the state of Ohio acquired Sandy Beach and surrounding acreage for the first state park on Lake Erie. State officials predicted that the end of World War II gas rationing would bring crowds to the area. East Harbor State Park opened in 1949, and the prediction was proven correct.

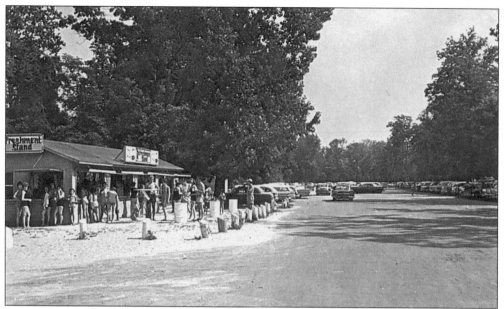

For some years a refreshment stand flourished near the beach. At times, the popularity of the beach puts parking at a premium.

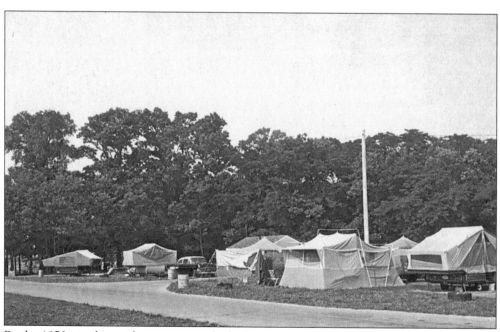

By the 1970s, trailers with pop-up tents had gained popularity over tents staked to the ground. By this time, East Harbor State Park offered 600 campsites coupled with hiking trails and a nature program.

Five

MARBLEHEAD
PENINSULA

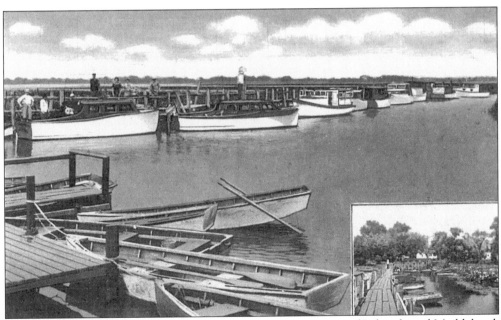

The Marblehead Peninsula is home not only to the communities of Lakeside and Marblehead, but also to many small housing developments. Channel Grove, pictured here in a 1930s vintage postcard, was one of the early developments that combined a marina with cottages. As the 21st century begins, much of the shoreline is occupied by housing developments, mobile home parks, or condominiums, all often coupled with boat docks.

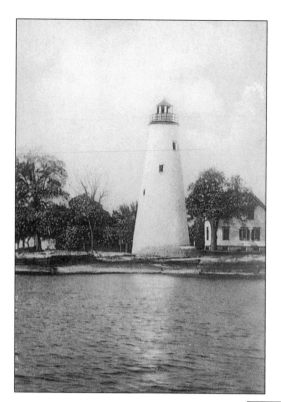

This image of the Marblehead Lighthouse and the keeper's house pre-dates 1897, when an additional height of 15 feet was added to the top of the light.

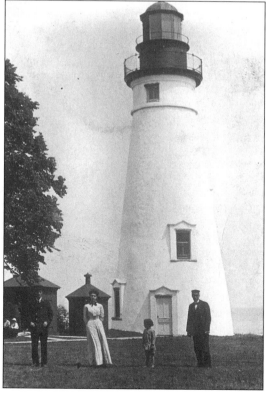

Edward Herman, the assistant keeper, is pictured c.1915 with an unidentified woman and child. Charles A. Hunter, on the right, was lighthouse keeper from 1903 to 1933. Kerosene was stored in the two small buildings to fuel the light before it was wired for electricity in 1923.

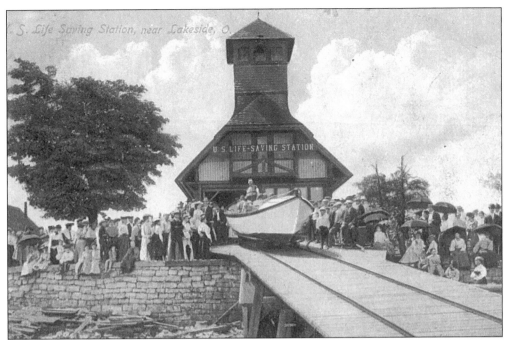

In 1876, a life saving station was established on the Marblehead Peninsula. Weekly practice sessions for launching rescue boats attracted admiring crowds in the 1890s. Before radio and radar, a lookout was stationed in the tower during navigation season while others patrolled beaches.

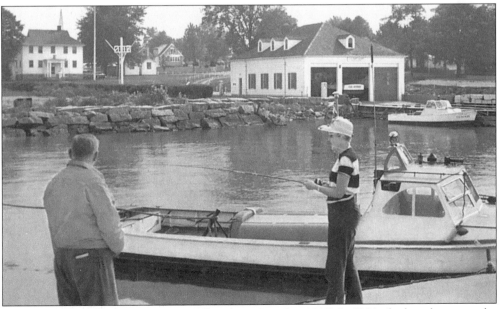

The life saving service became part of the Coast Guard in 1915. In 1921, the boat house on the right was constructed with Coast Guard crew quarters at the left. This facility served until a brick structure was erected in 1982.

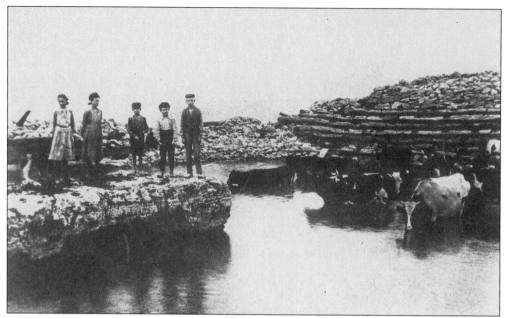

Several small quarry operations shipped limestone from the peninsula in the 19th century. Pictured is Gamble's dock, located just outside Lakeside's east gate at the bend of Harsh Road. Owner William Gamble, son of the founder of the Proctor and Gamble Company, and his wife were prominent Lakesiders.

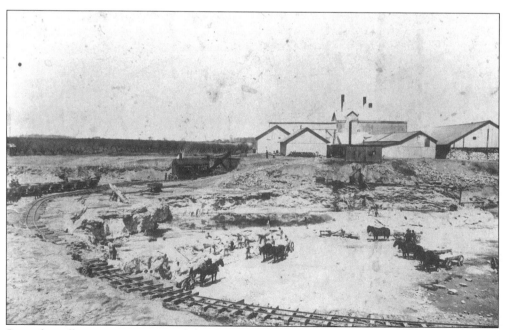

Several small quarries were consolidated into one operation when purchased in 1887 by the Kelly Island Lime and Transport Company. Originally a labor-intensive industry, over 1,500 men were employed at the Marblehead quarry in the early 1900s.

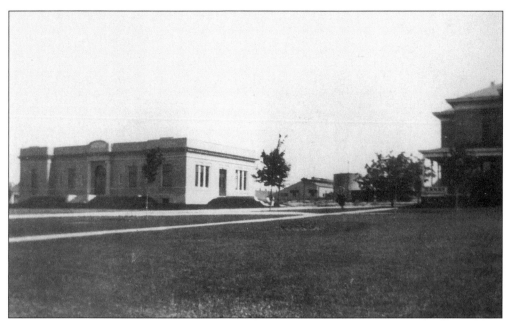

In 1914, the Kelly Island Lime and Transport Company built the hospital on the left for employees and their families. Originally a residence, the building on the right housed KILT offices, the telephone exchange, and the Lakeside and Marblehead Railroad office. Years later, the hospital became the Standard Slag office building.

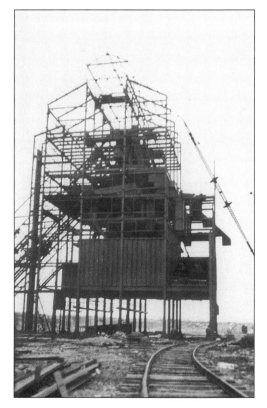

An advance in mechanization was made in 1922 when the Kelly Island Lime and Transport Company built this stone crushing and sorting operation. Galvanized steel sides were added to complete the structure.

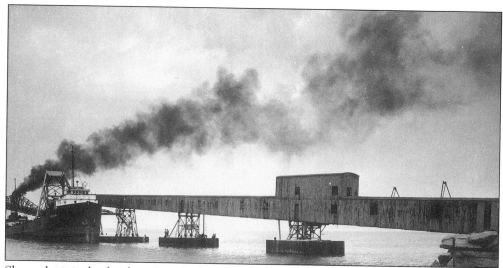

Shown here is the freighter *Sumatra* being loaded with crushed limestone. In 1968, freighters were loaded at the rate of 2,000 tons per hour. The covered conveyer system was later replaced by an open conveyor from the quarry to the dock.

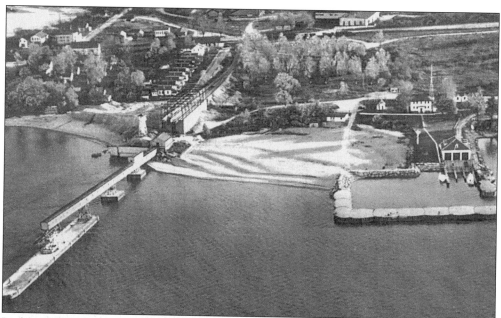

In this *c.*1940 aerial view of the Village of Marblehead, the loading dock appears on the left and the Coast Guard Station on the right. The row of houses that parallels the loading apparatus was known as millionaires' row because the quarry company provided them the luxuries of water and steam heat.

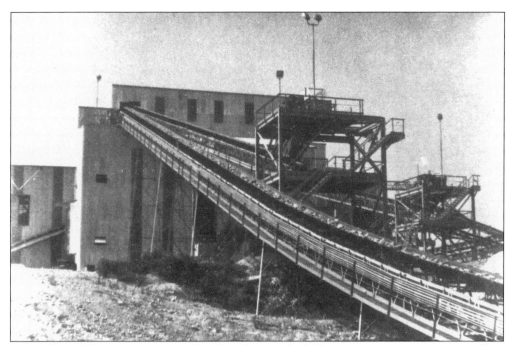

Ownership of the quarry was transferred to the Standard Slag Company in 1962. Two million tons of crushed and screened limestone were produced annually by 1968. The crushing and screening plant pictured here processed 800 tons of limestone per hour.

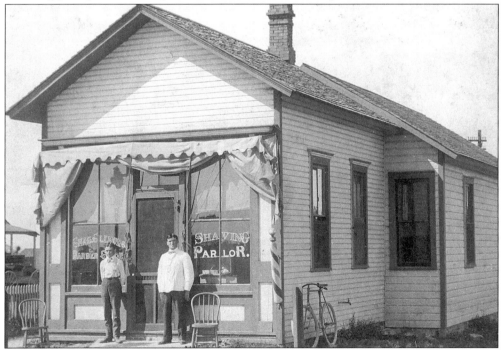

Around 1910, one of the businesses on Main Street in Marblehead was Charles Clemons's Barber Shop and Shaving Parlor. Standing in front of the building are Steve Ontko and Charles Clemons.

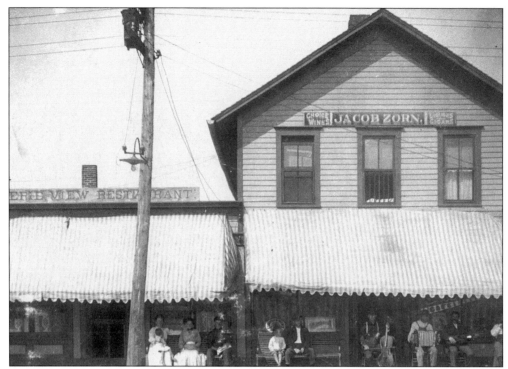

In 1909, Marblehead's Erie View Restaurant was adjacent to Jacob Zorn's place, which featured liquor and cigars. Band members at far right under the awning included Jake Zorn, Jake Voight, Gus La Rocque, and John Meyers.

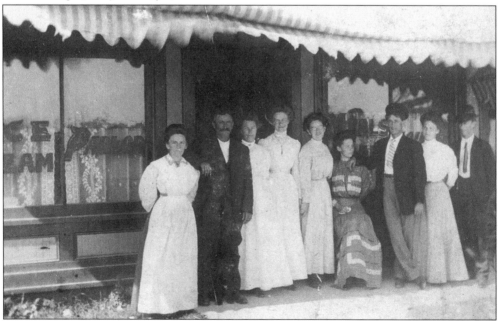

The group standing in front of the lace-curtained ice cream parlor c.1915 includes Anna Snyder Nuber, George Snyder, Emma Nuber, Elsie Brown Lublow, Lottie ?, Edna Nuber Myers, Walter Myers, Henrietta Nuber Vaughn, and Joe Vaughn.

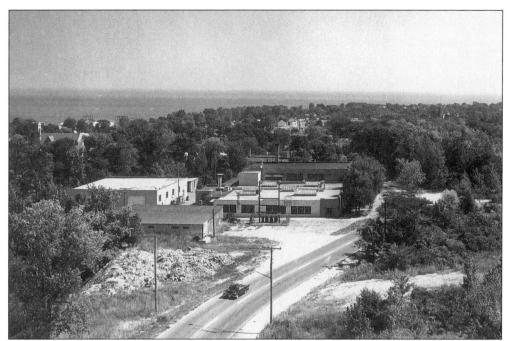

In 1930, Carl Biro Sr. incorporated the Biro Manufacturing Company, pictured here in the 1950s, to produce the meat cutting machine he invented. There has been both a national and international market for Biro meat cutting equipment for many decades.

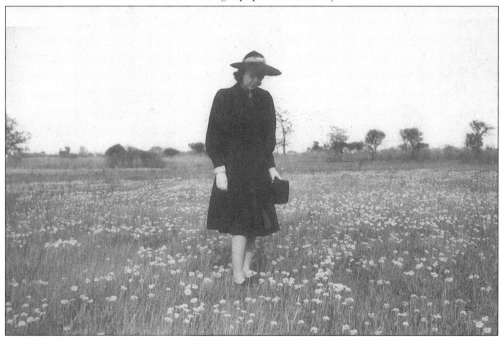

In 1941, Ruth E. Fiscus of Cleveland examines a field of Lakeside daisies (hymenoxys herbacea). She was joined by Colleen "Casey" Taylor of the peninsula in efforts to preserve this rare plant. In 1997, a State Nature Preserve was dedicated in honor of these two women on land donated by the LaFarge Corporation, current quarry owner.

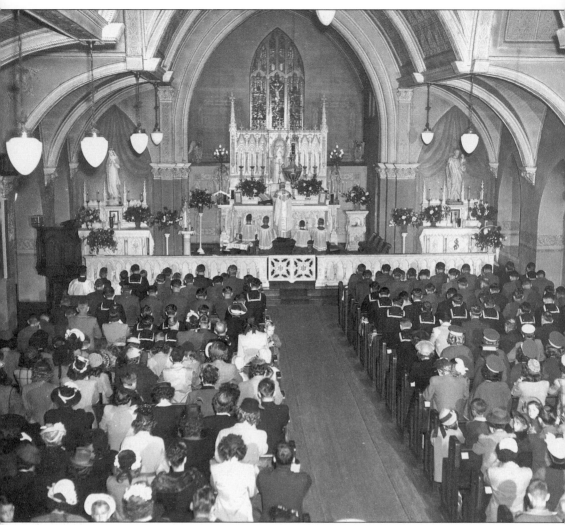

In mid-1946, when service men and women finally arrived home from World War II, a special Mass was held at Marblehead's St. Joseph's Roman Catholic Church, the cornerstone of which was laid in 1916. Father August Schaefer officiated. The congregation had outgrown previous church buildings since the first was constructed in 1867. Veterans organizations and their auxiliaries have played an important part in community life on the peninsula, making the Veterans of Foreign Wars Hall one of Marblehead's chief social centers. Other churches in Marblehead include First United Church of Christ, Holy Assumption Orthodox, St. John Lutheran, and St. Mary Byzantine Catholic Church. Each sanctuary elegantly reflects the traditions of that faith.

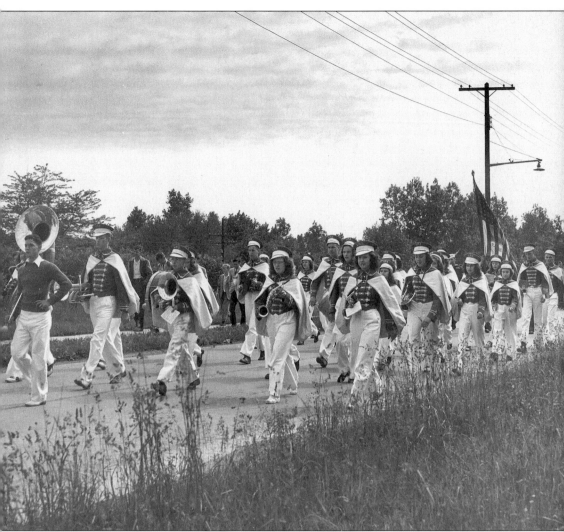

On the day of the special Mass in 1946, a parade honored returning veterans and those who had lost their lives. The band for Lakeside High School, now known as Danbury High School, preceded the veterans in the parade. Interestingly, until the changes precipitated by World War II, communities often found it inappropriate for young women to march and wear slacks in a band. Though school boards in Ohio were not required to have high schools until 1914, a high school in south Lakeside graduated its first class in 1892. By 1912, a new facility was built in Lakeside, which served the peninsula until the current high school was erected on Route 163.

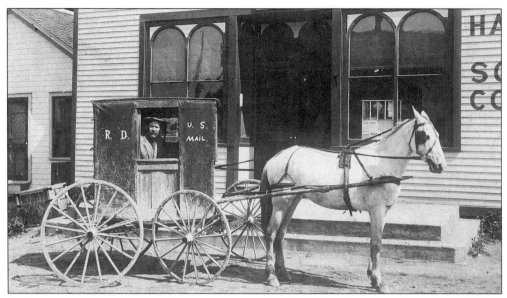

Danbury is an unincorporated community on the Sandusky Bay near the railroad bridge. In 1910, George Turner was the mail carrier for Danbury's own post office, located in Roth's Store.

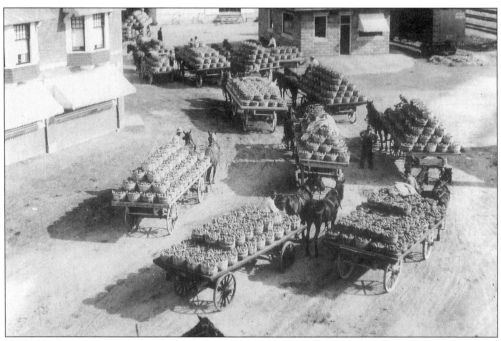

Fruit growers on the peninsula and Catawba often brought their peaches or other orchard products to the Danbury Fruit House, where fruit was shipped by train to many locations across the country.

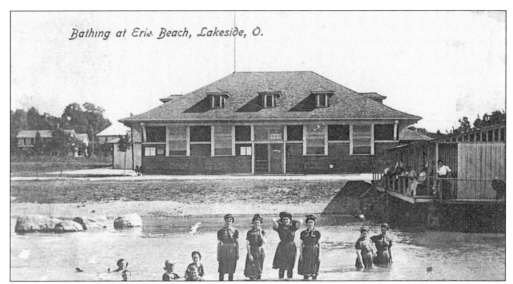

Located a short distance west of the Lakeside fence, the Erie Beach Resort offered facilities for swimming, sailing, and picnics. Early 20th century advertising claimed it was a good place for church and Sunday School picnics, but Lakeside ultimately dominated that market.

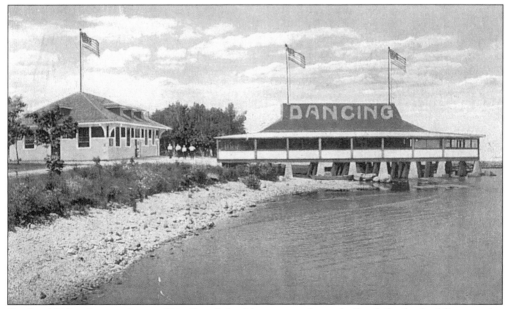

By the 1920s, the pavilion at Erie Beach had become a dance hall, while the building on the left served as a drugstore. Decades later, Lakeside Marine Inc. converted the drugstore to an office. When the pavilion was demolished, sections of dance floor were used in Lakeside Marine buildings.

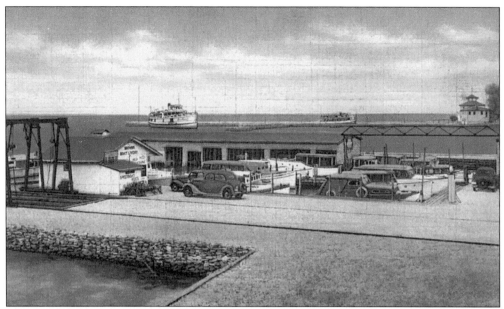

Just to the west of the Lakeside fence, Brown's Boat Livery offered charters and speedboat rides as well as dock space. This 1939 scene shows the *City Of Hancock* in the background arriving at the Lakeside dock with the *Lakeside III*, owned by the Browns, tied up at the dock.

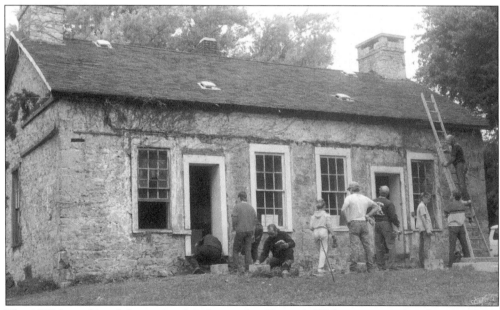

The 1809 log cabin of the peninsula's first settler, Benajah Wolcott, was replaced in the 1820s by a house of local limestone. Wolcott was the first keeper of the Marblehead Lighthouse from 1822 until his death in 1832. In 1989, the Ottawa County Historical Society acquired the title to the house. This picture shows volunteers in the early stages of restoring the county's oldest house.

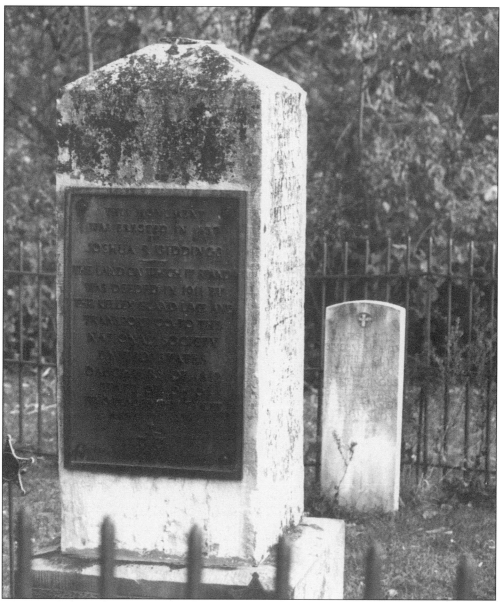

In September of 1812, the War's first land battle in Ohio was fought on the peninsula opposite Johnson's Island. U.S. troops from Fort Avery (near Milan, Ohio) were engaged in a skirmish with British-backed Native Americans. Settlers who had fled before the battle returned months later to bury the remains of eight American casualties in a mass grave. During the 1850s, Joshua R. Giddings, a teenager during the battle and later a U.S. Congressman from Ohio, had the large monument pictured here erected. The Giddings monument listed only three names, perhaps because the three had been his friends and were the only names known to him. A smaller stone was added later with all eight names. In 1911, the Kelly Island Lime and Transport Company transferred title to the property on which the monument is located to the National Society of the United Daughters of 1812. This organization erected the fence and maintained the site until 1991, when title was transferred to the Danbury Township Trustees. The Township added a parking area and now maintains the monument.

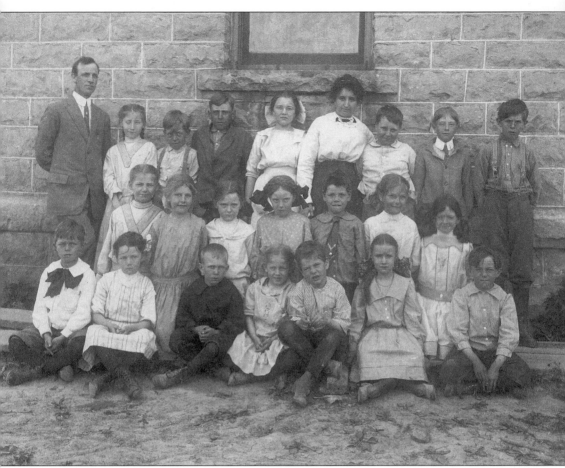

Before school consolidation, a Danbury Township School was located at the intersection of what is now Route 163 and Buck Road. Those attending in 1912 were (front row) unidentified, unidentified, William Wahlers, Chloe Netherland, Robert Ahrens, Elsie Schwick, and Alfred Beerman; (middle row) Emma Bruns, Lorena Miller, Inez Ipson, Mary Schultz, Charles Ahrens, and Doris Wahlers Titsworth; (back row) teacher Clarence Muggy, Marie Bruns, Frederick Wahlers, John Schultz, unidentified, teacher Lydia Powell Meek, ? Reidmeir, John Tewers, and Lenard Anderson. The school building was torn down soon after this photograph was taken. It is said that some of its materials and equipment went to the school on Port Clinton Eastern Road, which is now the Danbury Township Hall.

Six

JOHNSON'S ISLAND

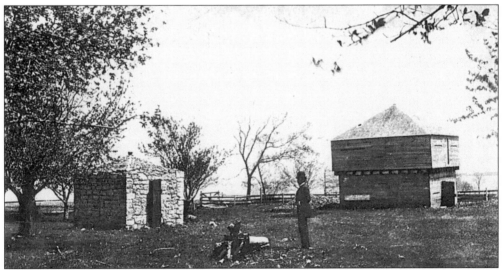

L.B. Johnson (not to be confused with the American president) leased his island for an annual rent during the Civil War as a prison site for captured confederate soldiers. At war's end, the military auctioned movable items, and only a powder magazine and block house remained by 1900. Artifacts of prison life continue to be found through present-day archaeological excavations.

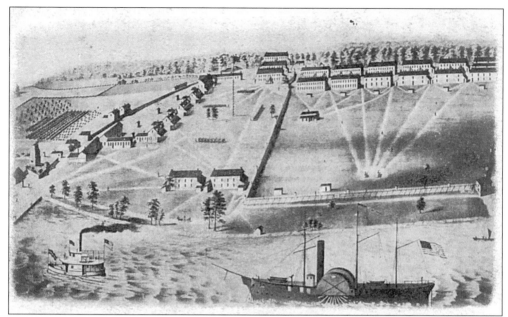

This 1865 drawing illustrates the prison for Confederates on Johnson's Island. On the right are two-story barracks that could house 2,500 prisoners. Outside the stockade on the left were quarters for U.S. troops who guarded the prisoners. The U.S.S. *Michigan*, a gunboat in the foreground, was kept near the island to intercept any attempt to free the prisoners.

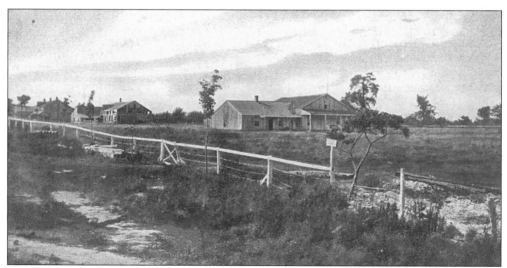

After the conclusion of the Civil War in 1865, officers' quarters remained standing for a few years, but were eventually dismantled for the lumber. Some may have been towed to the mainland over ice on the lake.

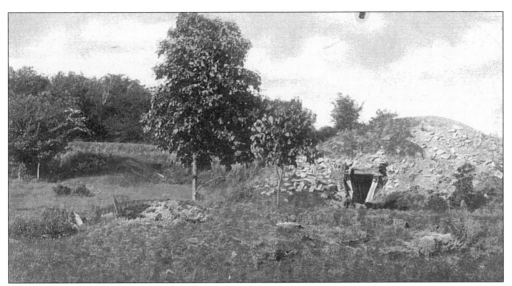

Visible in this 1890s photograph is a powder magazine and section of an earthworks embankment built to secure prisoners. Johnson's Island was designated a National Historic Landmark in 1990.

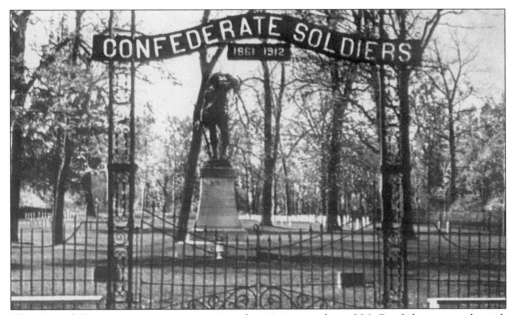

The United States government maintains the cemetery where 206 Confederates are buried. Deteriorating wood markers were replaced in 1890 by those made of Georgia marble by a group of the state's businessmen. A Confederate soldier monument was dedicated in 1910 by the United Daughters of the Confederacy. Services are held each Sunday of Memorial Day weekend to honor those who wore both the blue and the gray.

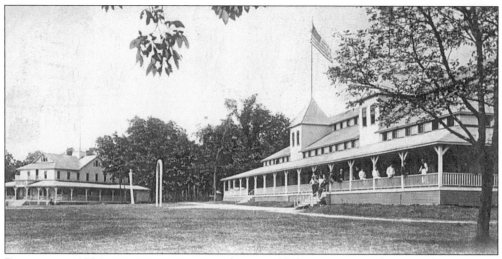

Beginning in 1894, two attempts were made to establish a resort on Johnson's Island, and by 1905, the area featured a hotel and pavilion. In order to avoid competition, the owners of Cedar Point purchased the Johnson's Island resort and suspended its operation.

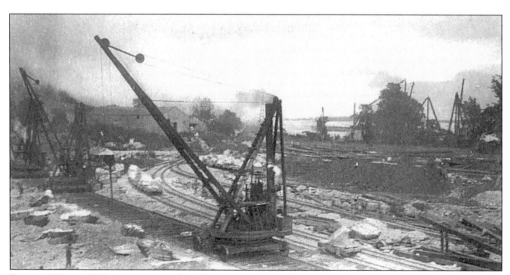

From 1901 to 1908, approximately 150 men were employed in a quarry operation on Johnson's Island. A small community for quarry workers included a store and a school. Some years later, a second attempt to establish a quarry was undertaken.

Seven

LAKESIDE

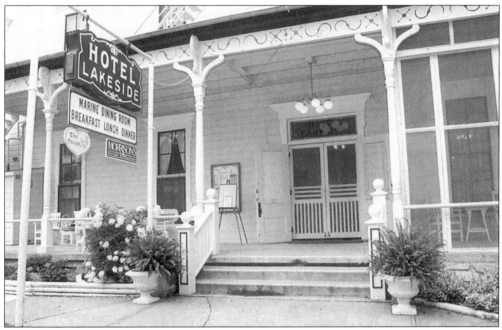

Lakeside, a community of 850 homes, is administered by a nonprofit corporation related to the United Methodist Church. People of all faiths enjoy its amenities, including Hotel Lakeside, pictured here in the early 1990s.

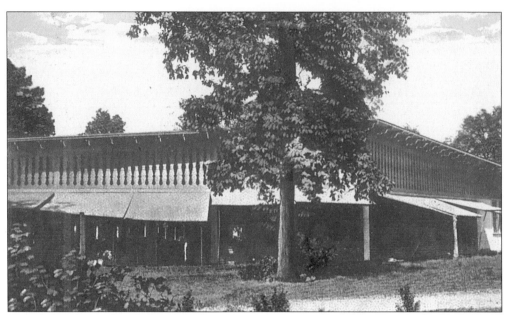

Since Lakeside was founded in 1873, the old auditorium—a place for religious, educational, and cultural programs—has stood at the heart of the community. The structure originally consisted of a roof on posts, but by the 1890s, lift-up sides were added.

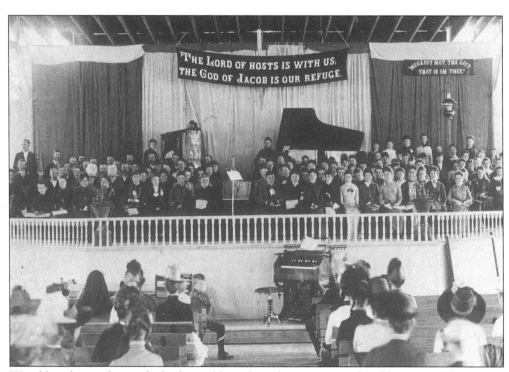

Wood benches with straight backs could not have been very comfortable seating. There were also complaints of difficulty seeing around women's large hats. By 1928, the need for a larger, more modern auditorium prompted the demolition of the structure shown here.

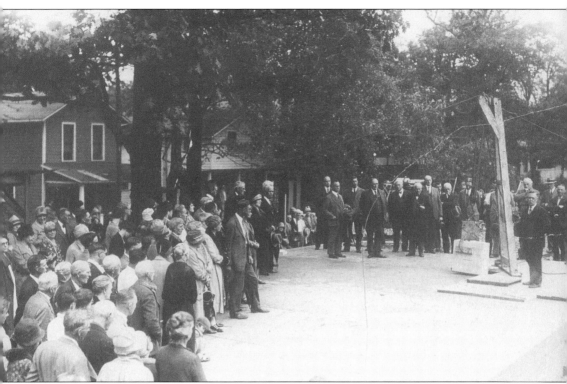

Against a backdrop of Central Avenue cottages, a crowd gathers in October of 1928 to watch the cornerstone being laid for the new Central Auditorium. The speaker was Ernest C. Wareing, editor of the *Western Christian Advocate*. The group of men in the center are Lakeside trustees with clergyman Dr. J. W. Dowds, the tall man in the middle. Also participating in the program were Peter J. Slach, a Cleveland banker who was president of the board of trustees, and A. L. Hoover, manager of Lakeside from 1926 to 1946. Just months after completion of the new auditorium, the stock market crash of 1929 led to the Great Depression. Hoover invested not only administrative skill, but also much of his personal fortune, in solving Lakeside's resulting problems. In 1949, after his death, the auditorium was re-named in Hoover's honor.

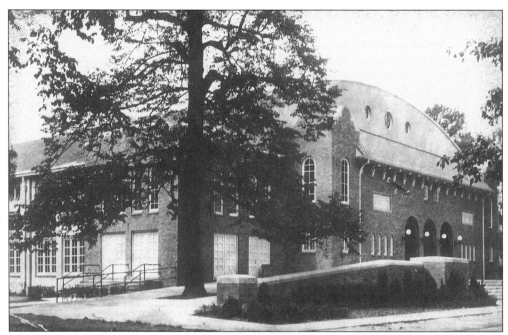

The new auditorium, with a seating capacity of 3,000, has had on its stage outstanding preachers, musicians, and dramatists. Included among them have been such names as Amelia Earhart, Drew Pearson, Mary McLeod Bethune, J. C. Penney, Marian Anderson, and Norman Vincent Peale.

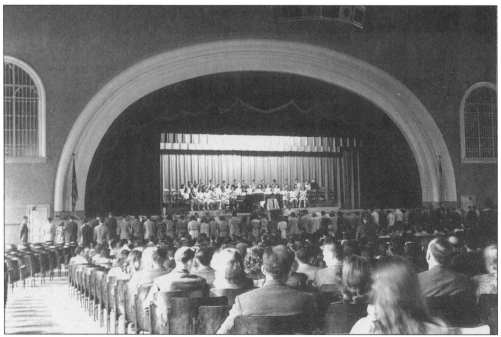

During the 1940s, a Methodist youth group known as the Epworth League held a service in Hoover Auditorium. In addition to Sunday morning church services, Hoover Auditorium is used every night during the summer for cultural programs or entertainment.

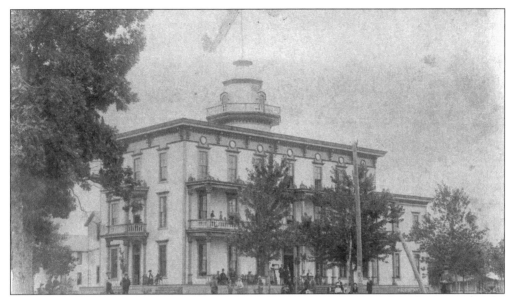

In the 1880s, Hotel Lakeside is pictured with an attached two-story privy and an annex at the rear constructed in 1879. The original section was built in 1875, making it the oldest hotel in continuous operation in Ottawa County, and probably the oldest on Lake Erie.

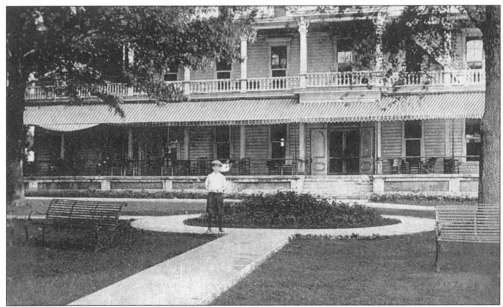

By the 1920s, the hotel had mellowed in appearance. Chairs lined the first floor porch and gaily colored awnings gave it a festive air. Imagine renting a second floor room with people walking on the balcony outside your window.

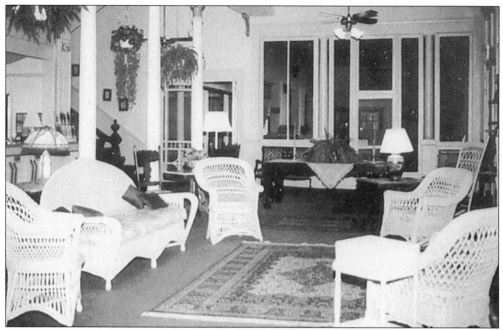

A proposed plan in the 1970s to tear down the hotel and build a modern motel created community controversy. As a result, the Lakeside Association adopted a renovation plan for the hotel as an alternative. A recent image of the lobby showcases the end result, with the registration desk on the left and dining room at the rear.

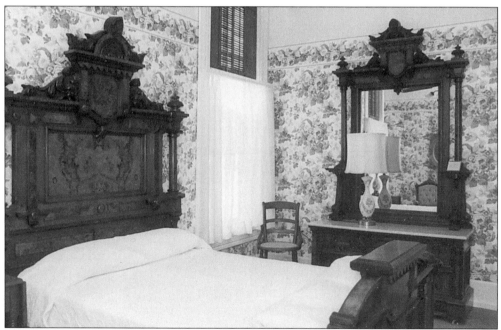

By the 1980s, Hotel Lakeside's 90 rooms were renovated and furnished with antiques. This room's furniture once belonged to Charles Foster, governor of Ohio from 1880 to 1884. He spoke at Lakeside several times and had a summer home on Middle Bass Island.

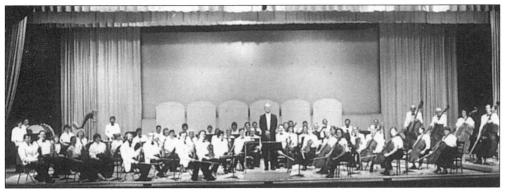

Lakeside is a gated community where a summer fee entitles the ticket-holder to use recreational facilities and attend the daily religious, educational, and cultural programs. The Lakeside Summer Symphony, which plays several concerts per week, has been in residence during the month of August since 1964. Robert Cronquist has served as director since 1970.

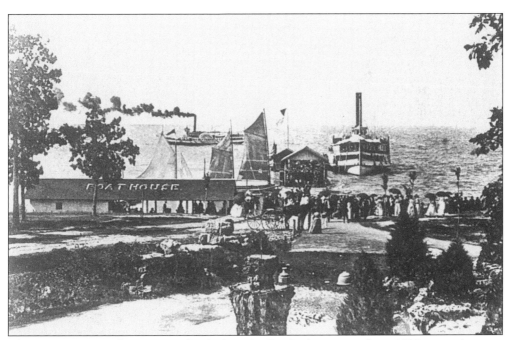

The steamer *Metropolis* arrives at the dock as the *Pearl* is leaving in this *c.*1889 scene. Arriving passengers paid a gate fee at the building on the dock, as the first pavilion was not erected until 1909.

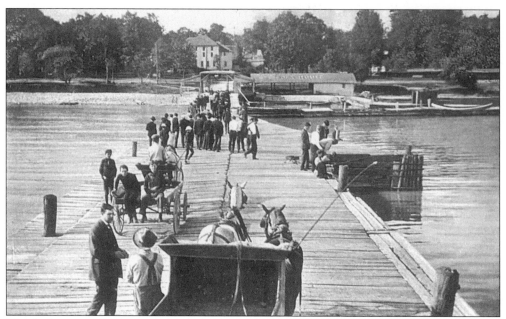

The dock pictured here was originally constructed of wood. Because freight and baggage arrived by boat, horses and wagons often parked on the dock. The house in the background is the McDonald House with Hotel Lakeside just visible on the right.

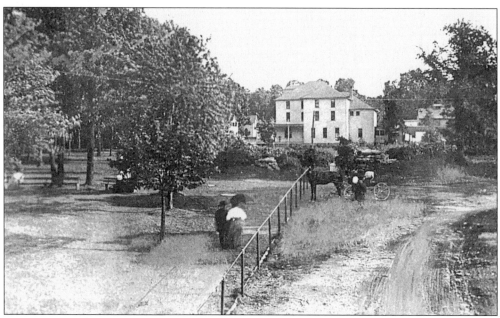

Just across Maple Avenue from the Hotel Lakeside, a large rooming house was erected in 1895 by Mrs. A.C. McDonald, but fire destroyed the building in 1905. Notice the long hitching post from the McDonald House to the dock. Except for brief stops, horses had to be tethered south of Seventh Street.

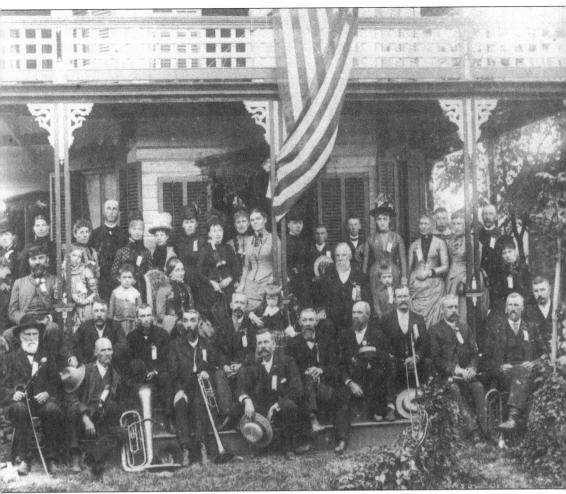

Lakeside was the location of several reunions held by former President Rutherford B. Hayes for the 23rd Ohio Volunteer Infantry Regiment, which he commanded during the Civil War. In 1887, veterans of the regimental band were joined by friends on a cottage porch at Third and Sycamore. Seated to the right and left of the flag are General Hayes and his wife, Lucy Webb Hayes. Samuel Gill, a Lakeside founder, can be spotted in the back row on the left. His wife, Mary Alexander Gill, is the woman in a light dress next to the flagpole. The man in the cap seated in the middle row left next to the post is E. C. Griswold, then president of the Lakeside Company as well as manager of the hotel for several years. There is speculation that Hayes held reunions at Lakeside because the ban on liquor kept the men from becoming rowdy.

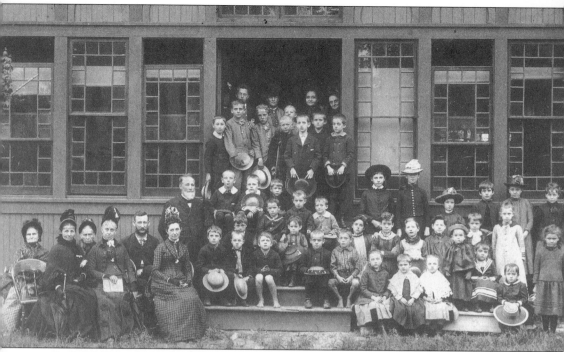

In 1887, Captain Alva Bradley's widow had Bradley Temple built in memory of her husband, the owner of one of the largest fleet of boats on the Great Lakes. Soon after the temple's completion, Mrs. Bradley asked that the facility be used primarily for children's programs, such as the Sunday School gathering assembled here. Located at Third and Cedar, Bradley Temple remains a center for children's activities more than a century later. Alva Bradley, once a Lorain County farm boy, acquired a fortune and eventually lived on millionaires' row in Cleveland as a contemporary of John D. Rockefeller. In his younger years, he befriended the Edison family of Milan, Ohio, and the Edisons named their son Thomas Alva in his honor.

When Lakeside was platted in the 1870s, no one could have anticipated that families would eventually arrive by automobile. Lots 33 feet wide proved adequate, eliminating the need to clear tree stumps from the narrow streets.

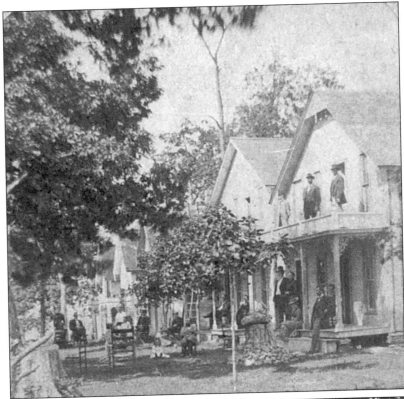

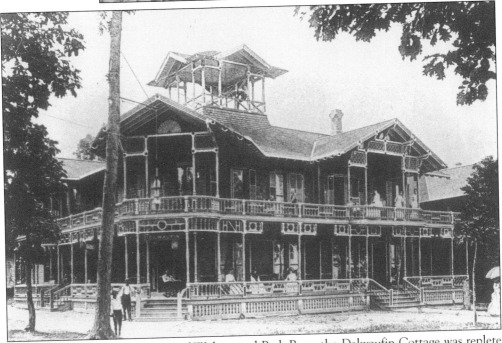

Built in the 1880s at the corner of Walnut and Park Row, the Delwaufin Cottage was replete with Victorian gingerbread. The cottage, in actuality three apartments owned by families from Delta, Wauseon, and Tiffin, was part of the block destroyed by fire in 1905.

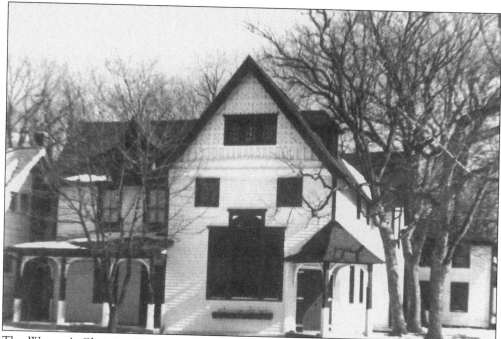

The Women's Christian Temperance Union occupied a building on the northeast corner of Fifth and Central from 1889 until 1960. Advocating such causes as women's suffrage and banning the sale of liquor, the WCTU brought such speakers as Frances Willard, Susan B. Anthony, Dr. Anna Howard Shaw, and Carrie Chapman Catt to the area. This photograph was taken in the snow not long before the building was demolished.

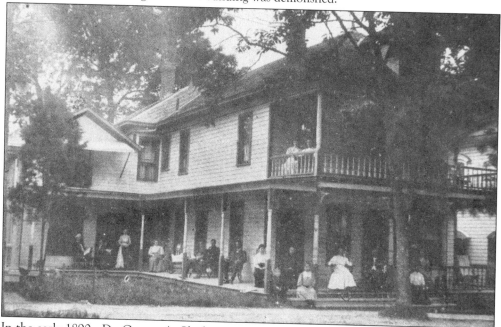

In the early 1890s, Dr. George A. Slack operated his medical office out of this building. After his death in 1897, the Slack House was rented for office space and overnight rooms, but gave way to the construction of the Green Room at Fountain Inn in 1962.

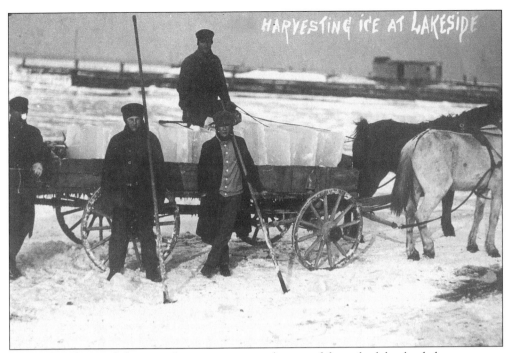

Before the advent of electric refrigeration, ice was harvested from the lake, loaded on a wagon, and stored for summer use, as depicted here *c.* 1890. The poles or pikes were used to push the blocks through water. Blocks were then loaded for transport to the ice storage house on the lakefront at the end of Oak Avenue.

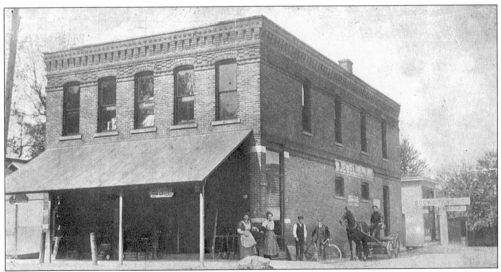

The brick store at the corner of Walnut and Second Street was built in 1892 by Barney Jacobs, one of the founders of Lakeside as well as a Civil War veteran, Port Clinton businessman, and German immigrant. The buildings at the rear were located where the Fountain Inn parking lot is today.

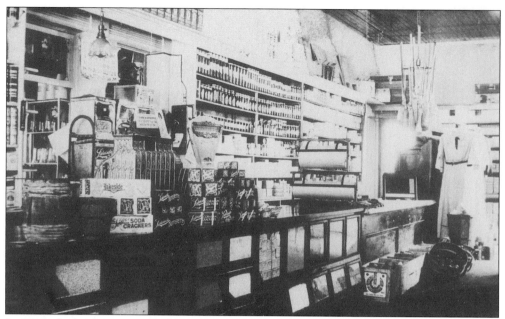

In 1915, the brick store stocked a wide variety of goods, including groceries, furniture, fishing tackle, shoes, and women's dresses. With space later divided into as many as four shops, the building has housed such businesses as a confectionery, hardware store, R.G. Grill, rock shop, real estate office, men's store, women's store, and various gift shops.

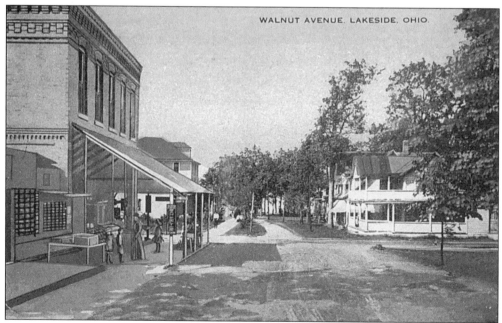

Much has changed since this c. 1920 glimpse of Walnut Avenue looking towards the lake. The small shop on the left now has an outdoor postcard display, and the house on the right was removed to make room for Orchestra Hall.

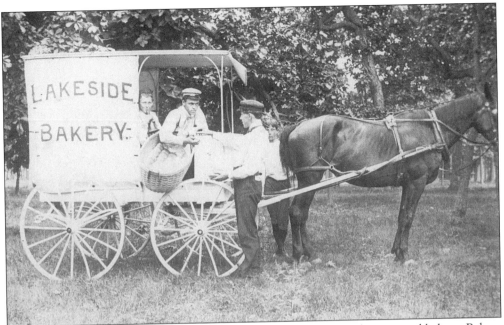

John and Dan Carroll owned a grocery store, general store, dry goods store, and bakery. Bakery deliveries were made by horse and wagon. The grocery store, after being destroyed in 1905 by a fire that demolished the block bound by Maple, Walnut, Second, and the lakefront, was ultimately rebuilt at Second and Maple.

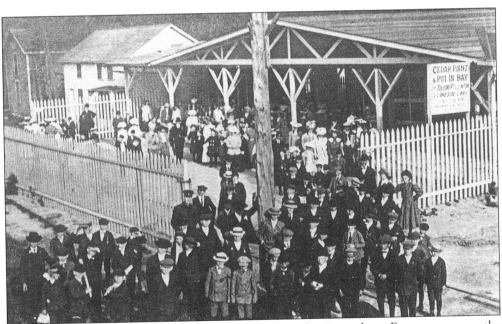

Around 1910, a large group arrived at Lakeside on the interurban. For many years, the conductor collected the Lakeside gate fee during the ride from Port Clinton to Lakeside. A cottage now occupies the site of the interurban station at the southeast corner of Fifth and Maple.

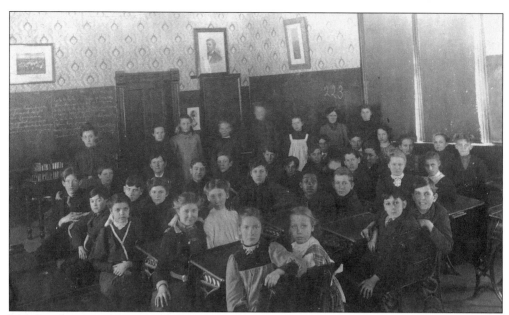

Miss Pettibone, visible on the left in the back row, was the teacher of this class at the Lakeside school c.1911. The school, a two-story frame building located on what is now route 163 in South Lakeside, was abandoned not long after this picture was taken.

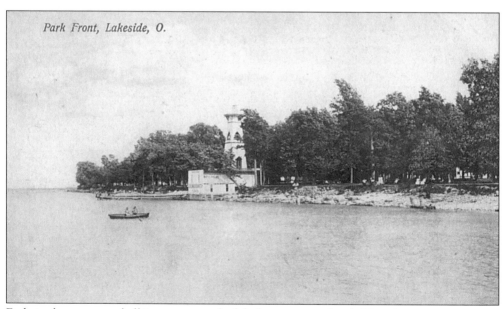

Park Front, Lakeside, O.

Early in the century, a bell in a tower on the lakefront rang to signal rising times, meeting times, quiet hour, etc. The bell tower housed a drugstore and ice cream store, as well as a bath house for changing into bathing suits. A short wooden dock that extended from the base of the tower provided the swimming area.

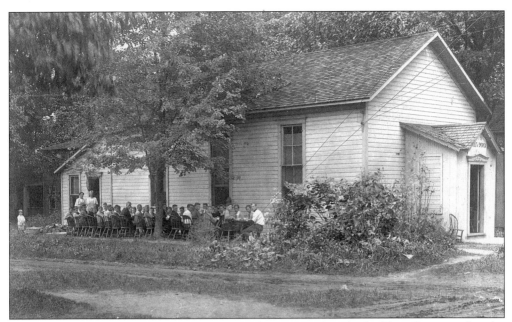

Here, *c.* 1915, a Boy Scout troop from Lorain shares a meal in the building that served as the Methodist Church until 1900. It then became Ladies Aid Society Hall, and was used by both church and community groups. Since the 1960s, the building has been home to the Heritage Hall Museum.

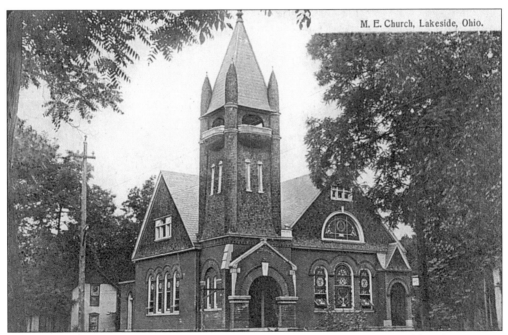

M. E. Church, Lakeside, Ohio.

This building was purchased by the Methodists in 1900 when the frame building became too small. It had been built in 1892 by the Grand Lodge of Ohio of the Independent Order of Good Templars, a temperance organization. The Templars had run out of money before the interior was completed.

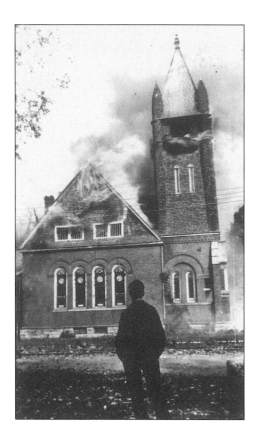

An onlooker watches helplessly as flames engulf the roof and steeple of the church in October of 1929. Except for the parsonage next door to the church, everything in the block was destroyed by fire.

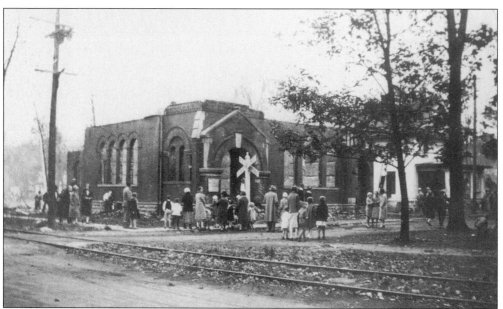

People came to survey the damage done by the church fire. Notice the railroad crossing sign and the interurban tracks on Fifth Street. Church services were held in Orchestra Hall until a new church was built in 1953.

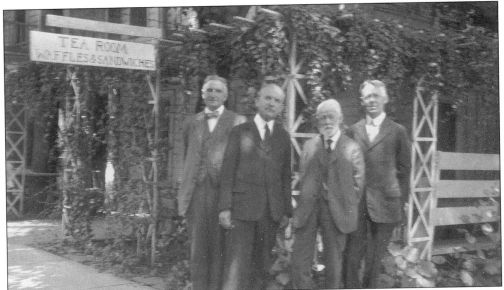

In 1927, the Mayflower Tea Room, which became the Abigail Tea Room in the 1930s, specialized in serving waffles. The four professors shown here include Dr. J.Y. Simpson from Edinburg, Scotland, Dr. Rollin H. Walker from Ohio Wesleyan University, Dr. William N. Rice from Wesleyan College in Connecticut, and Dr. Edward L. Rice from Ohio Wesleyan University.

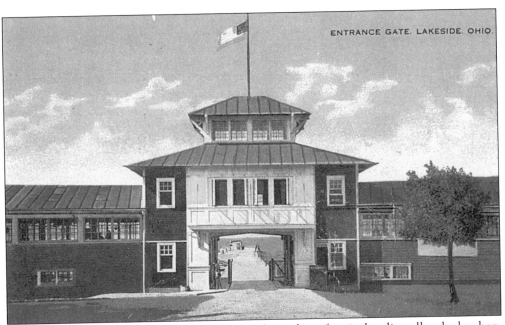

Over the years, the first pavilion, built in 1909, housed a cafeteria, bowling alley, barbershop, boat house, and gift shops. Gate tickets were sold at the dock for as long as people arrived by steamboat.

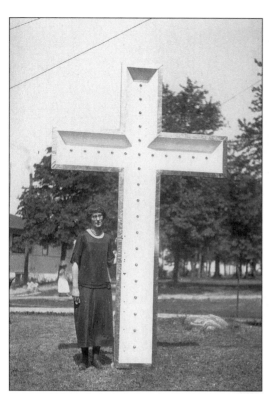

A lighted cross was mounted on top of the first pavilion in 1925 in memory of A. B. Jones, Lakeside's manager from 1914 to 1924. His widow, Ida Smith Jones, who was manager in 1925 and 1926, is shown with the cross before it was mounted.

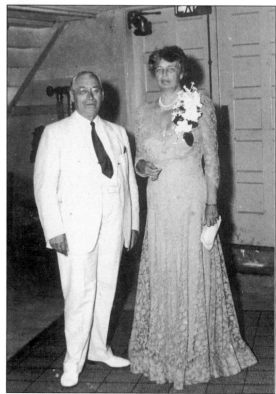

When she spoke in 1940 to an overflow auditorium audience, Eleanor Roosevelt was escorted backstage by Lakeside manager A. L. Hoover. Mrs. Roosevelt refused to discuss whether her husband would seek nomination for a third term.

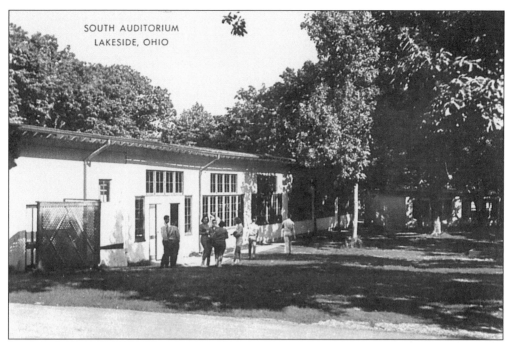

Shown here c.1962, this building, originally called German Auditorium, was used by the state's German-speaking Methodists during summer months from 1883 to 1933. Re-named South Auditorium, it is now used for youth conferences and a variety of other purposes.

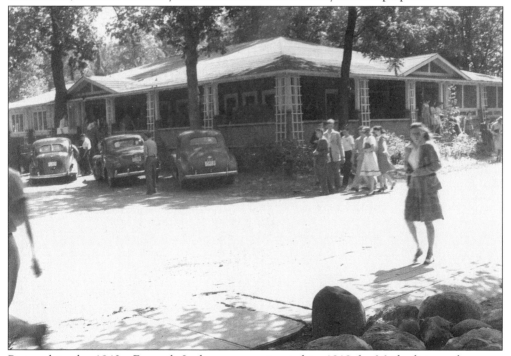

Pictured in the 1940s, Epworth Lodge was constructed in 1919 for Methodist youth groups known as the Epworth League. In 1999, it was rededicated for use as the C. Kirk Rhein Jr. Center for the Living Arts.

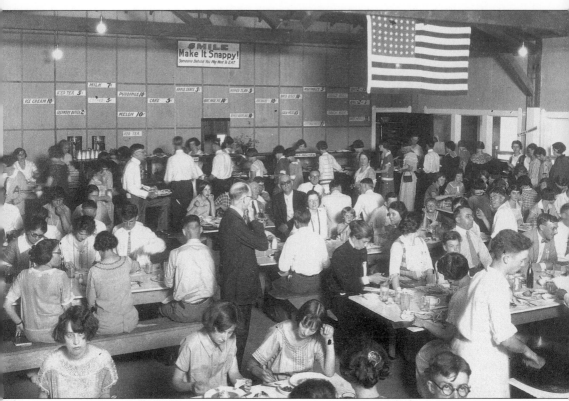

For many years, Epworth Lodge was used as a dining hall for youth groups. This 1920s picture shows the cafeteria line and those seated at tables. In 1963, Wesley Lodge was constructed as a dining hall with a much larger seating capacity. The 1920s prices posted on the wall included such items as cold meats for 15¢, vegetables for 3¢, pepper slaw for 5¢, creamery butter for 2¢, milk for 7¢, and cake for 5¢. Ever since the early years of the 20th century, Lakeside has been visited annually by hundreds of young people belonging to a variety of youth groups. Dormitory facilities of various sizes, auditoriums, an outdoor worship center, and recreational facilities make Lakeside an ideal place for young people to hold conferences, band camps, and other educational events.

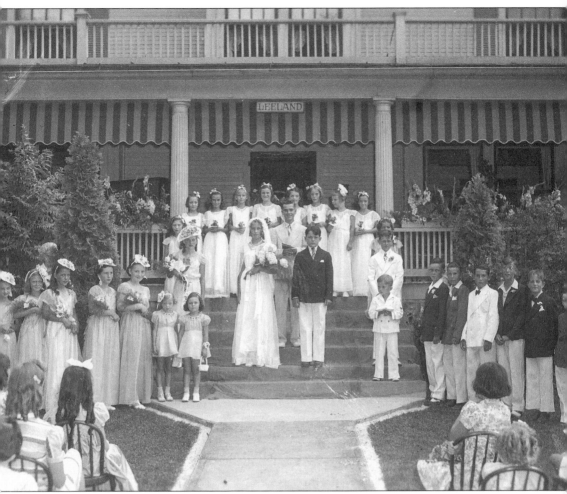

During the 1930s and 1940s, Mrs. T. M. Dolin's yard at 506 East Third Street was often the site of fund-raisers for the Women's Club. This mock wedding in 1948 was billed as the Wedding of the Flowers. Patsy Harris was the mock bride, Richard Waering the groom, and Allen Ellery the preacher. On the steps behind the bride is a double octet composed of Nancy Corbett, Ileene Blondell, Barbara Ingram, Natalie Mitchell, Marilyn Harris, Harriet Lord, and Barbara Ellery. The maid of honor was June Swinnerton and the best man Dan Sebring. Bridesmaids were Janice Broderick, Marie Tilton, Joan Dole, Pattie Faris, and Jo Ann Amerine. Flower girls were Mary Jane Sherk and Bonnie McMinn. Bob Lucas was the ring bearer. Ushers were Bud Christie, Hobart Porter, Henry Adler, Bob Tressle, Richard Smith, and an unidentified boy. Tom Aigler played the piano.

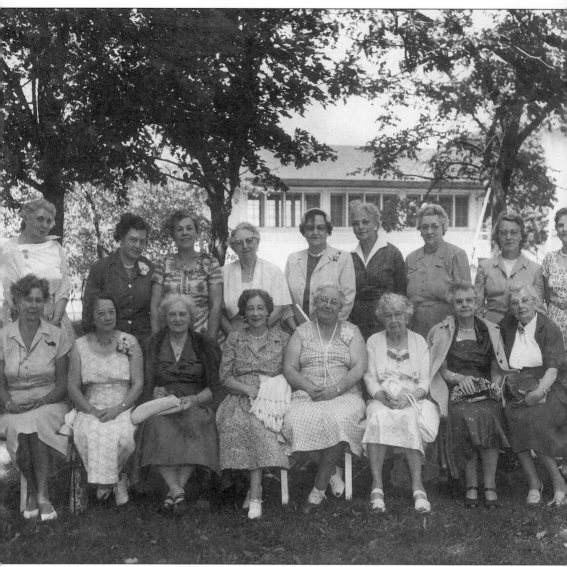

Founded in 1928, the Women's Club is an important summer organization. Board members in 1956 are pictured as follows: (front row) Dr. Helen Elkins, Mrs. C.E. Cronenbarger, Mrs. Robert Witchner, Miss Alta Smith, Mrs. Ada Park, Mrs. W.H. Bachman, Mrs. R.W. Kauble, and Miss Anne Weidmann; (back row) Mrs. Albert Miller, Mrs. Lee Cherry, Miss Eleanor Durr, Mrs. Ed Yeasting, Mrs. Herbert Thompson, Mrs. E.S. Braithwaite, Mrs. S.F. Edwards, Mrs. Rachel Theiss, and Mrs. Charles Wolfe. The 1956 board members launched a home tour that has become an annual event attracting hundreds of visitors annually to view Lakeside cottages or homes. There are activities six days a week at Green Gables, the club house at 161 Walnut Avenue where men may become associate members. Saturday morning story hours are held for children, and a lending library is available to the community.

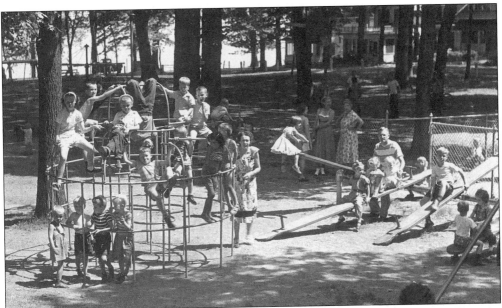

A supervised playground for small children pleases parents and children. This 1953 scene at the playground near the lakefront features Kenton Row cottages in the background.

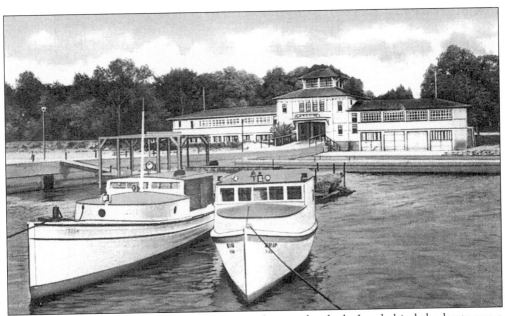

For a few years, privately-owned boats were tied up at the dock. Just behind the boats was a short dock reached by ramp from the main dock which was used to secure speed boats. A decision was eventually made that Lakeside would not be a marina, effectively banning private boats.

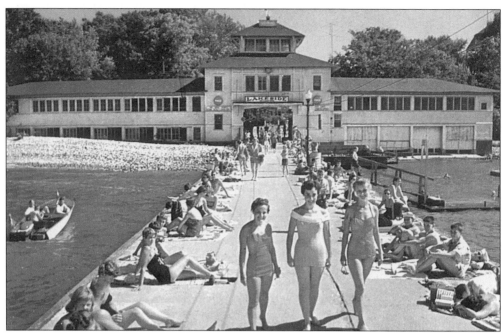

After the end of the passenger boat era, the dock became the place for swimming and sunbathing. Shown in the foreground of this 1956 picture are Nancy Wainwright Caldwell, Becky Stockham Presti, and Laura Jo Dalton. The first pavilion is visible in the background.

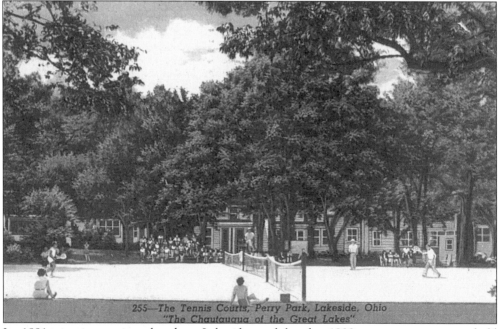

255—The Tennis Courts, Perry Park, Lakeside, Ohio
"The Chautauqua of the Great Lakes"

In 1891, tennis was introduced to Lakeside, and by the 1930s, tournaments were held with Ohio and out-of-state teams. Spectators viewed this 1950s game from bleachers in front of Plum Avenue cottages. Additional courts and a tennis pavilion have since been added on Sixth Street.

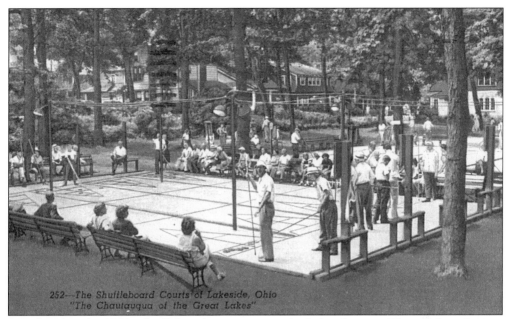

252—The Shuffleboard Courts of Lakeside, Ohio
"The Chautauqua of the Great Lakes"

Introduced in the 1920s, shuffleboard remains a popular Lakeside sport. The number of courts has been substantially increased since this 1957 picture. National tournaments have been held since 1968, and an international tournament was held in 1997.

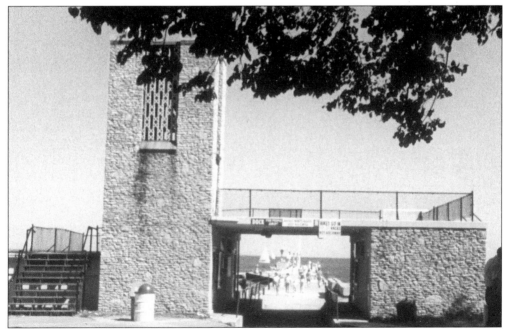

The original pavilion was replaced by this modernistic structure in the early 1960s, itself succeeded in the 1980s by one designed more compatibly with Lakeside's designation on the National Register of Historic Places.

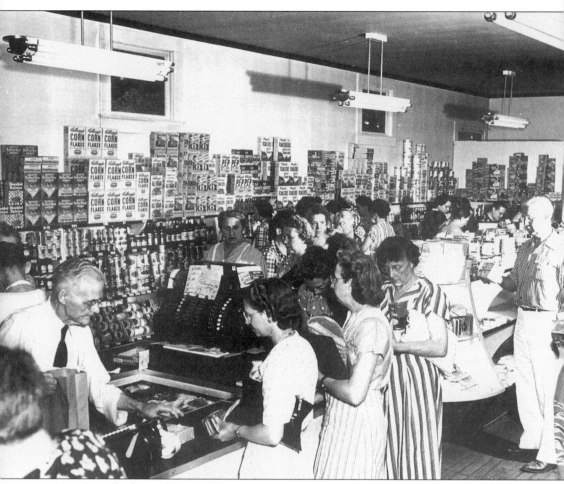

Dan Carroll, the cashier in this c.1945 picture, entered the grocery business in 1898 and was joined by his brother John in 1902. Their wood frame store at Second and Maple Avenue, along with the entire block, was destroyed by fire in 1905. The brothers built a new concrete block building at the same location. Though John died in 1946, Dan continued in business until 1949. The Carroll Building is now divided into several shops and owned by the Lakeside Association.

Eight
BASS ISLANDS

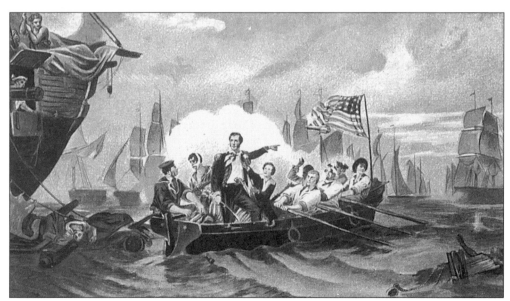

William Powell's 1857 painting shows Commodore Perry transferring from his damaged flagship during the battle of Lake Erie in 1813. Fought just off the Bass Islands, there are many reminders of the battle on the islands. Their celebrations target less the defeat of the British in the War of 1812 than the nearly two centuries of peace along the United States and Canadian border.

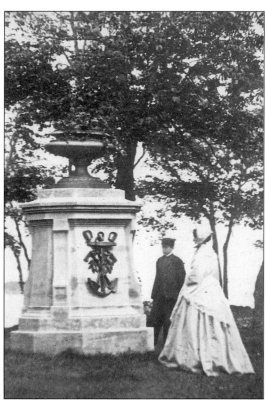

In September of 1813, a decisive battle of the War of 1812 was fought just off the Bass Islands.

U.S. naval forces under the command of Oliver Hazard Perry defeated the British. The first monument to memorialize the victory was erected by Jay Cooke on Gibraltar Island soon after he purchased the island in 1864.

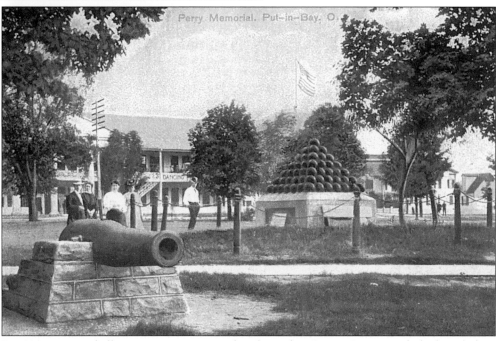

In 1899, a cannonball monument was erected in the park at Put-in-Bay to mark the burial place of three American and three British officers killed in the battle of Lake Erie. This monument was reconstructed in 1914 after their remains were moved to the Perry Monument.

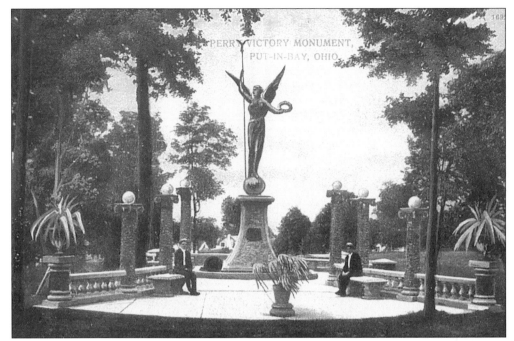

In 1907, a bronze victory monument was erected on the grounds of the Hotel Victory. After destruction of the hotel by fire, the statue fell into a state of neglect and was donated to a scrap metal drive during World War II.

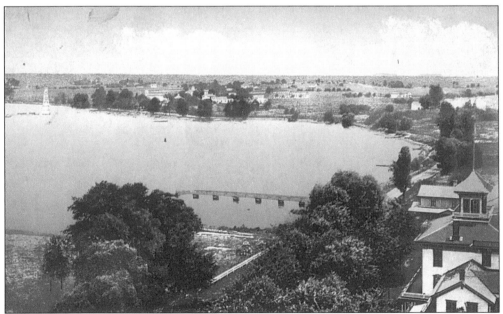

Various groups talked for decades about building a large memorial. Just beyond Put-in-Bay's Beebe House, shown here in 1905, is the narrow area between the bay and lake where the victory monument was eventually constructed.

Construction of the monument started in 1913, and opened to the public in 1915. Placed under the administration of the National Park Service in 1936, it was officially named Perry's Victory and International Peace Memorial.

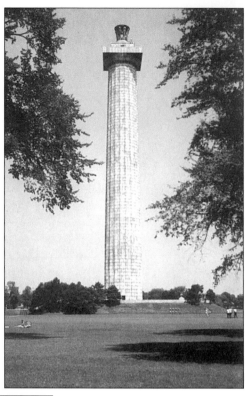

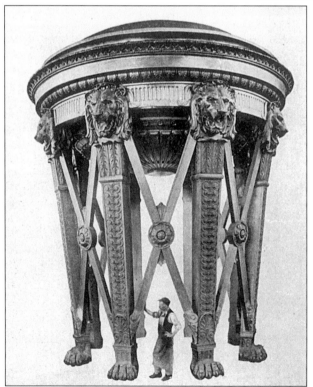

At 352 feet, Perry's Monument is the tallest Doric column in the world. Its bronze top is 23 feet high, weighs 11 tons, and is capped by a massive plate glass bowl.

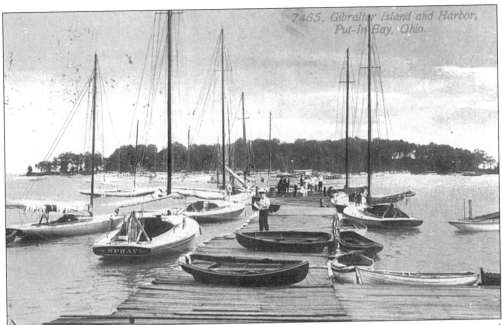

7465. Gibraltar Island and Harbor, Put-In Bay, Ohio.

Early in the 20th century, wood rowboats and sailboats were the principal craft for recreational boating, and annual regattas attracted crowds. Gibraltar Island serves as a backdrop for this seasonal image.

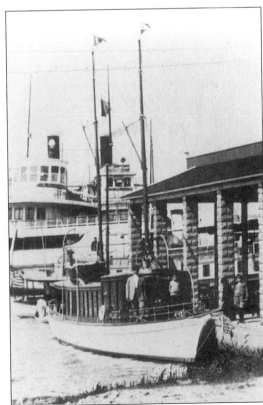

On July 18, 1907, the first ship-to-shore radio transmission in the world was made from the yacht *Thelma* at the finish line of the Inter-Lake Yachting Association regatta to Fox's Dock. The *Thelma* is pictured later tied up at the dock.

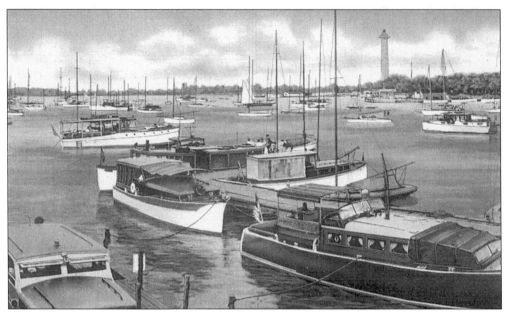

By the 1930s and 1940s, pleasure boats had become larger and more sophisticated. Their wood construction had a kind of beauty unmatched in later fiberglass boats. Perry's Monument is visible in the background.

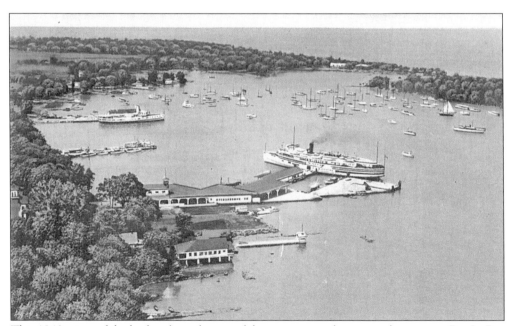

This 1940s view of the harbor from the top of the monument showcases the steamer *Put-In-Bay* at dock.

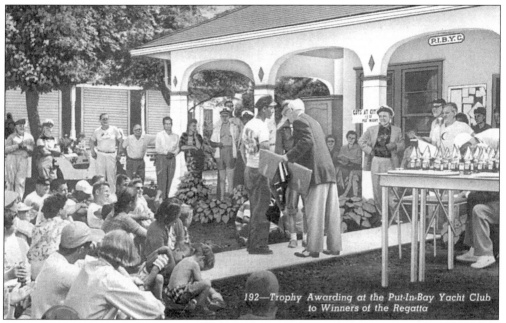

Regatta winners in 1952 were awarded trophies in front of the Put-in-Bay Yacht Club, constructed in 1924.

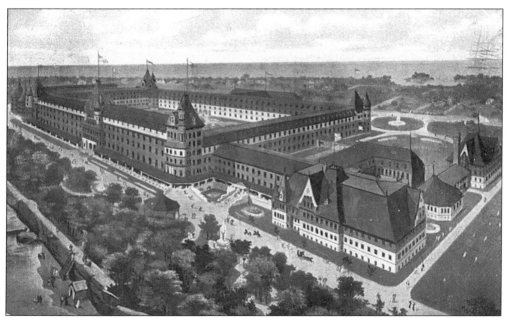

Built in 1892 with 600 guest rooms and dining rooms to seat 1,200, Hotel Victory was the largest summer hotel in the United States in its day. Destroyed by fire in 1919, its grounds are now occupied by South Bass Island State Park.

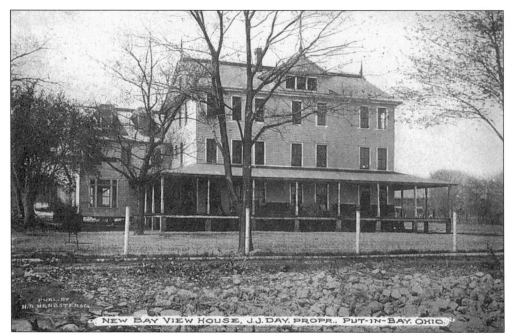

The Bay View House, built in 1870, was one of a number of small hotels in the area. In this 1910 picture, it was owned by John J. Day, who added the third story. The Put-in-Bay Yacht Club was eventually constructed adjacent to the hotel.

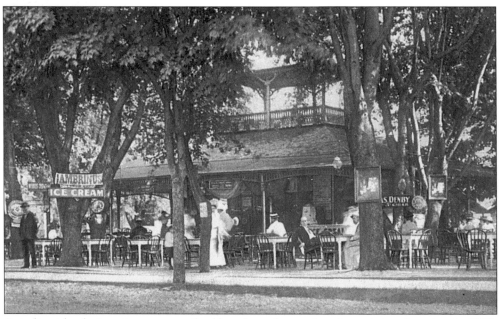

Sampling island wines, ice cream, or food has always been a favorite activity of tourists. In 1909, meals at Schraidt's Restaurant were thirty-five cents.

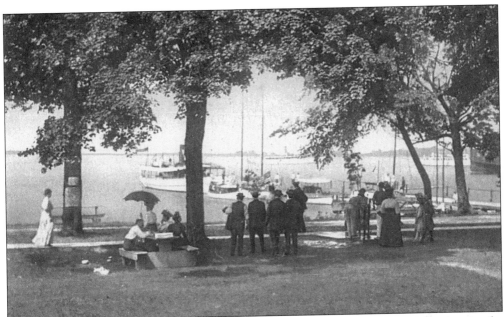

De Rivera Park, named for an early owner of the island, has always been a focal point for tourists. Joseph de Rivera St. Jurgo became the owner of South Bass, Middle Bass, Sugar, Gibraltar, Ballast, and Starve Islands in 1854 for a price of $44,000.

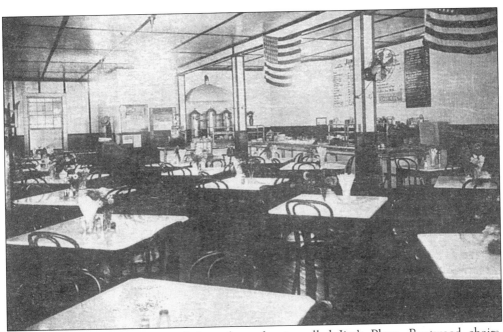

World War II era decor prevailed at the cafeteria called Jim's Place. Bentwood chairs, marbletop tables, coffee urns, flags, and one electric fan provided an ambiance not likely to be found again at Put-in-Bay.

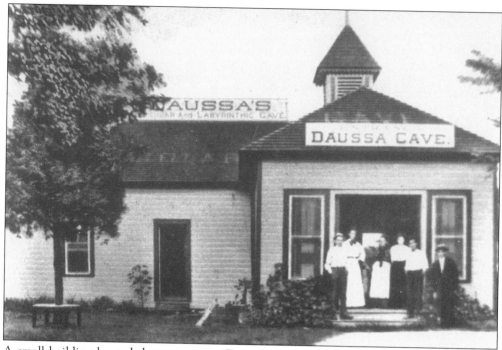

A small building housed the entrance to Daussa's Cave from 1899 to 1913. Later re-named Mammoth Cave, it is no longer open to the public. Numerous private caves on South Bass have long interested spelunkers.

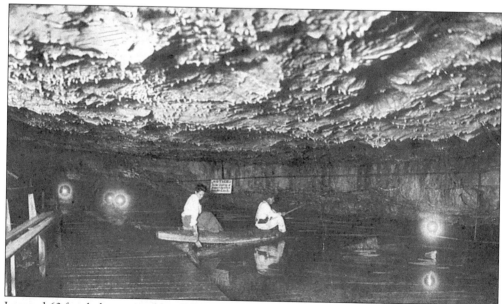

Located 60 feet below ground level, Daussa Cave included a lake from which a 600-foot tunnel led to a cavern and an exit. Falling rocks necessitated closing the cave in 1953. In recent decades, however, Crystal Cave at Heineman's Winery has been open to visitors.

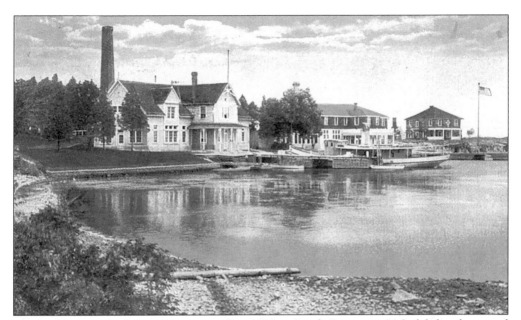

The building on the left was constructed in 1889 at Peach Point as a U.S. fish hatchery, and became part of the Stone Laboratory in 1940. The center building was a state fish hatchery, built in 1907, which burned in 1925. The cottage on the right has belonged to several generations of the Feick family. The tugboat *Oliver Hazard Perry* sits at the dock.

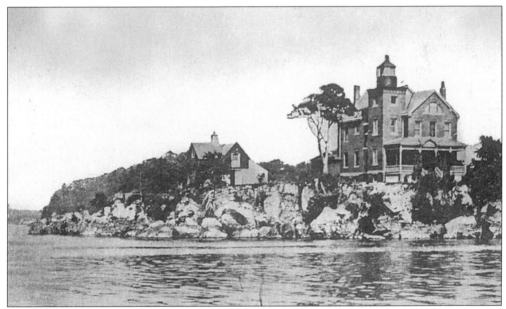

Built in 1897, the South Bass Island Light was in operation until 1962, when it was replaced by an automated navigational light on a steel tower.

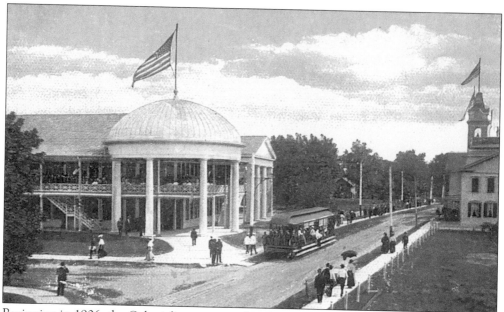

Beginning in 1906, the Colonial's restaurant, bar, bowling alley, and dance floor were tourist favorites. The trolley ceased operation soon after the Hotel Victory fire in 1919. The Town Hall cupola on the right was later removed, and the Colonial was destroyed by fire in 1988.

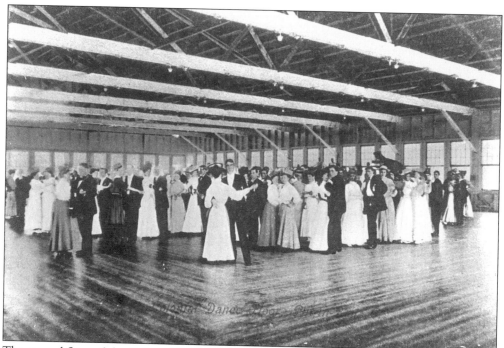

The second floor of the Colonial had an 18,000 square foot dance hall. Live orchestras played afternoons and evenings, attracting crowds like the one pictured here c.1915.

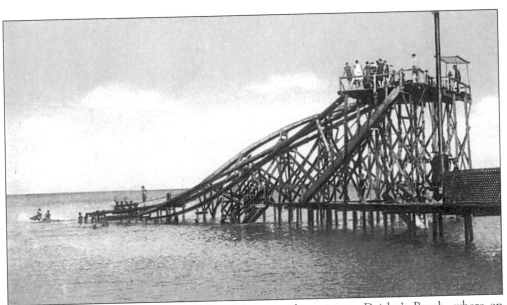

In 1904, a water toboggan with rubber slides coaxed tourists to Deisler's Beach, where an adjacent bath house offered 350 dressing rooms and 4,000 bathing suits for rent.

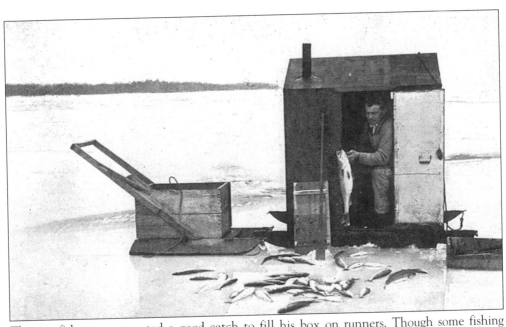

This ice fisherman expected a good catch to fill his box on runners. Though some fishing shanties were a little more commodious, the fisherman appeared to be successful.

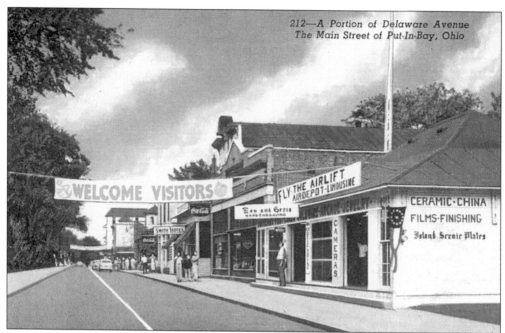

212—A Portion of Delaware Avenue
The Main Street of Put-In-Bay, Ohio

In the 1960s, tourist brochures described Delaware Avenue as "the little Paris of the Lake Erie Islands." The Smith Hotel, built in the 1880s, had previously been the Gill House, Hotel Oelschlager, and Bon Air. The building in the foreground was torn down and replaced by the Cargo Net.

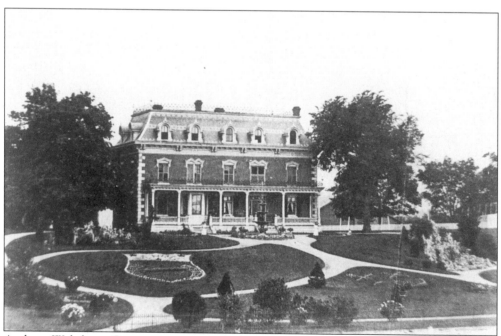

Andrew Wehrle, a German immigrant, built a winery on Middle Bass Island in 1865. A pavilion built a few years later over the wine cellars drew crowds of tourists. Wehrle's home (shown here), an Ottawa County show place, was built next to the winery in 1871.

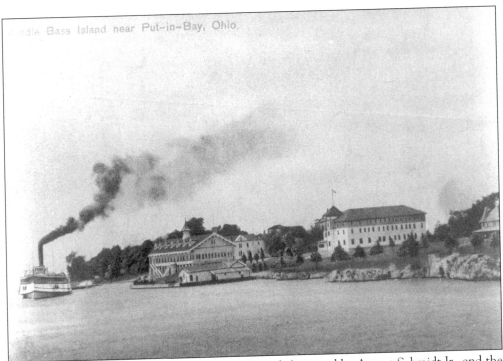

This 1908 image reveals the Schmidt Home (far right), owned by August Schmidt Jr., and the Golden Eagle Winery Pavilion (left). The Wehrle home had been destroyed by fire, and on its site, the Hill Crest Hotel (center) was constructed. Both the pavilion and hotel burned in 1923.

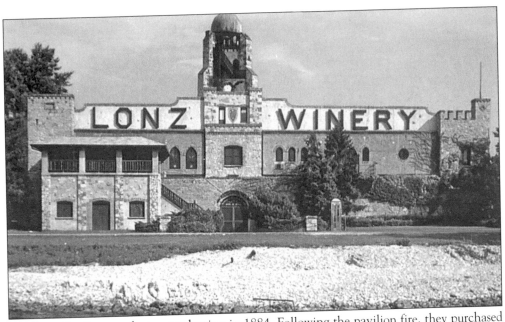

The Lonz family started wine production in 1884. Following the pavilion fire, they purchased the Golden Eagle Winery in 1926. After the repeal of the 18th Amendment ended Prohibition, the castle-like building was constructed in 1934 on top of the old Wehrle wine cellars.

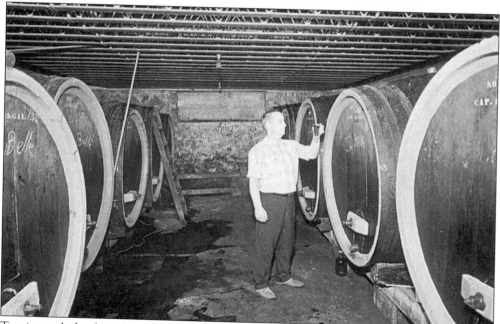

Tourists and island residents have enjoyed the products of the Heineman Winery on South Bass Island since 1896. Louis Heineman is shown here inspecting contents of 500 gallon casks in the 1950s.

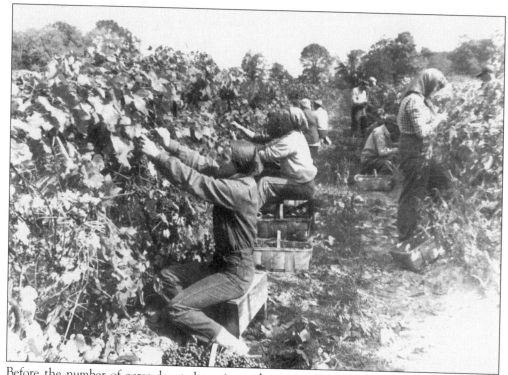

Before the number of acres devoted to vineyards was eroded by construction of new tourist facilities, picking grapes was a community event, as demonstrated in this 1940s image. Islanders offered to help and schools closed for two weeks so children could be involved.

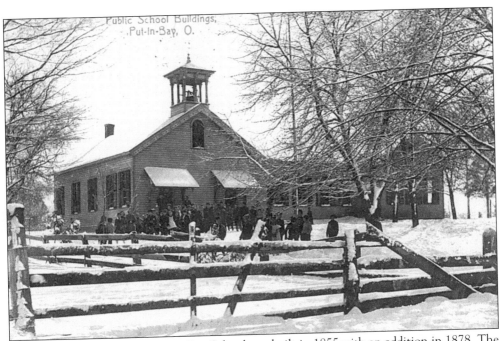

The original section of the Put-in-Bay School was built in 1855 with an addition in 1878. The school on the hill was replaced by a brick building in 1921. As one of the smallest school districts in the state, Put-in-Bay may have only one or two high school graduates per year.

Built in 1857, the North Bass Island school was replaced a century later by one of the few one-room schools still in operation. North Bass students go by plane to Put-in-Bay for high school. North Bass is officially designated by the U. S. Postal Service as Isle St. George. It is planted in the vineyards of the Meirs Wine Company and has no tourist development.

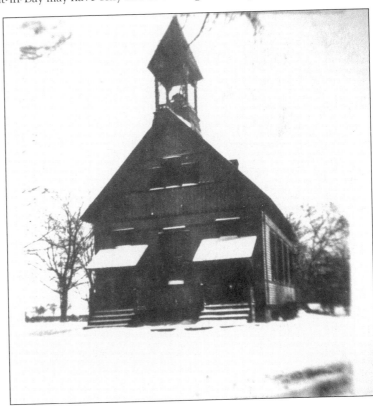

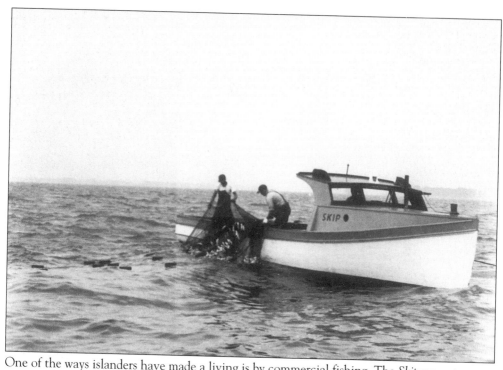

One of the ways islanders have made a living is by commercial fishing. The *Skip* was a trap-net boat with fish unloaded on deck. Engine exhaust went up a pipe assembled through the cabin roof.

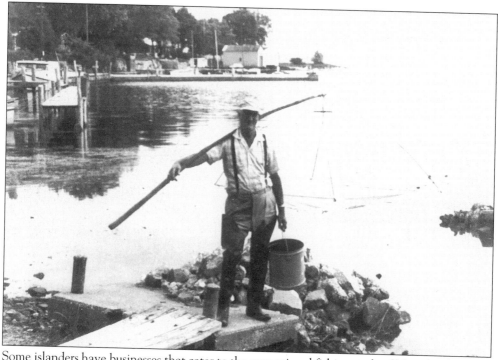

Some islanders have businesses that cater to the recreational fishing trade off the islands. In the 1950s, Charley Mahler, an island resident, seined for minnows to sell to tourists for bait.

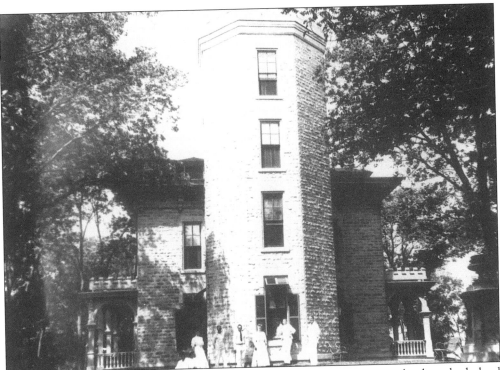

Son of Sandusky's first lawyer, Jay Cooke became a Philadelphia investment banker who helped the U.S. government finance the Civil War. He bought Gibraltar Island in 1864 and built an elaborate summer home now owned by Ohio State University.

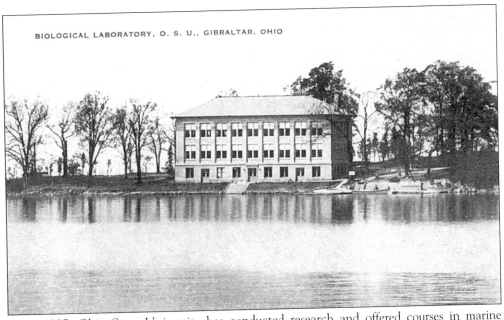

BIOLOGICAL LABORATORY, O. S. U., GIBRALTAR. OHIO

Since 1927, Ohio State University has conducted research and offered courses in marine biology and related sciences at Franz Theodore Stone Laboratory. In 1925, the son of the man for whom the lab was named donated six acres on Gibraltar Island to OSU for the facility.

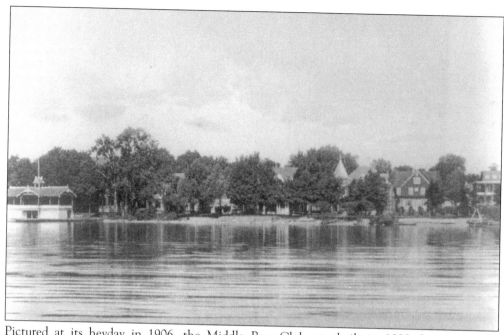

Pictured at its heyday in 1906, the Middle Bass Club was built in 1882, but eventually demolished in 1949. Members were wealthy socialites and famous politicians, some of whom built kitchen-free cottages nearby so that meals were taken at the club. The boat house is also visible at far left.

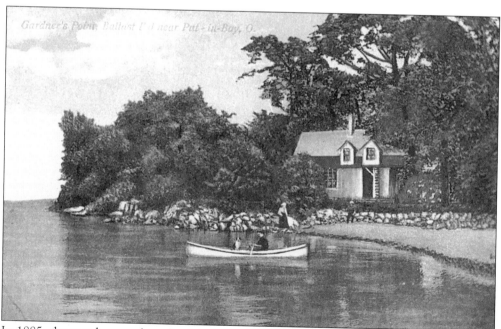

In 1885, the year he was elected to his first term as mayor of Cleveland, George W. Gardner helped organize the Western Canoe Association. A few years later, he was the first commodore of the Inter-Lake Yachting Association. Descendants still own his Ballast Island cottage.

Nine

TRANSPORTATION

It was a loss, not only for Island Airlines, but also for all lovers of the old Ford Tri-Motor planes, when this one crashed near the Port Clinton airport in August of 1972. People gathered to view the remains of one of the last of its kind. Nostalgia lingers despite the added comfort of newer makes and models.

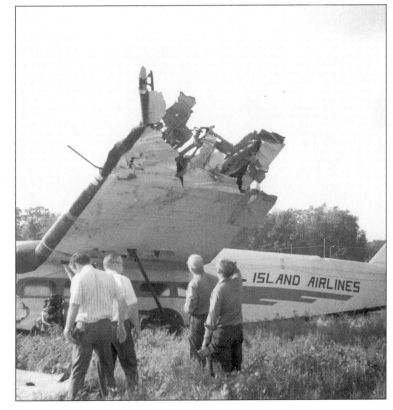

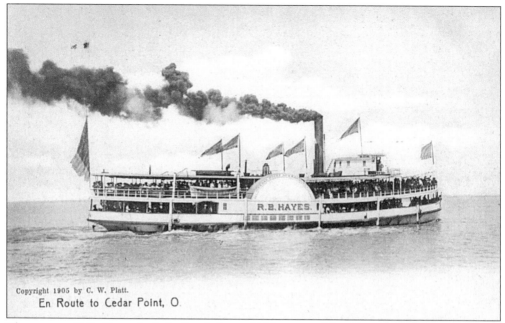

En Route to Cedar Point, O.

The steamer *R.B. Hayes*, built in Sandusky in 1876, operated locally until 1920. The boat was 134 feet long with a very shallow draft. Some years she carried passengers and freight from Sandusky to various peninsula docks. Excursions were occasionally run from Fremont to Cedar Point by way of the Sandusky River.

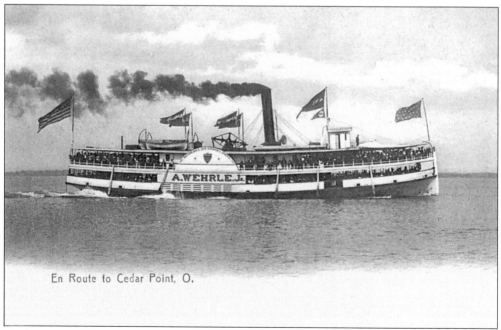

En Route to Cedar Point, O.

Andrew Wehrle of Middle Bass Island commissioned this steamer in 1889. Built in Sandusky, the boat was used by Wehrle both to bring passengers to his island resort and to ship wine. In 1891, she was sold to the Cedar Point Company.

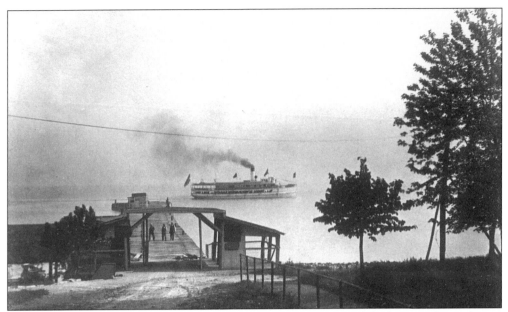

Built in 1901, the *Lakeside* was 128 feet long, and one of the first lake boats to have electric lights. Her steel hull was heavily plated to break through ice. Here, she is seen leaving the Lakeside dock. In 1917, the *Lakeside* was sold to the French government and cut down as a tug. World War I soldiers stationed overseas reported recognizing her in a French port.

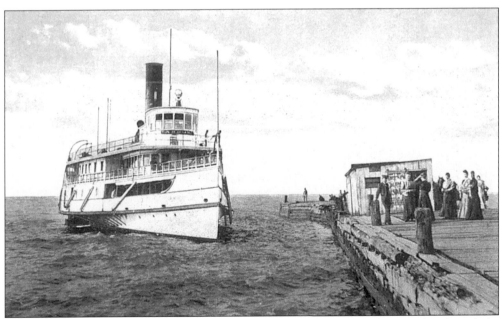

From 1895 to 1922, the *Arrow* claimed the island route from Sandusky to Lakeside and the islands. With a capacity of 800 people, the *Arrow* made several round trips per day during the summer months. Passengers either stayed over at resorts or connected with steamers to Toledo, Detroit, or Cleveland. Here, she is shown coming into the Lakeside dock.

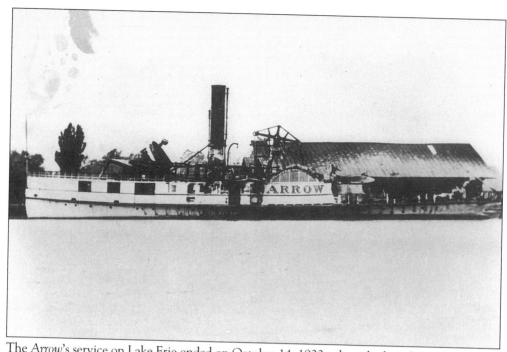

The *Arrow's* service on Lake Erie ended on October 14, 1922, when the boat burned at Put-in-Bay. She was rebuilt several times as a barge and ended her career under different names in other waters.

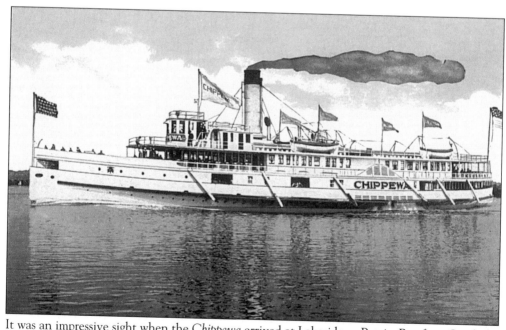

It was an impressive sight when the *Chippewa* arrived at Lakeside or Put-in-Bay from Sandusky with a dance band playing on deck. Converted from the U.S. Revenue Cutter *Fessenden*, the *Chippewa* occupied the island route from 1923 to 1938. The *Hancock* ran the route in 1939, when regular service from Sandusky came to an end.

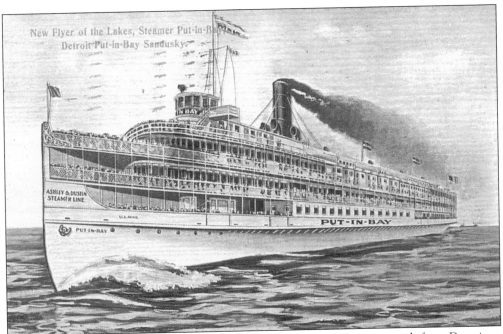

Most years from 1911 to 1948, the *Put-In-Bay* ran several round-trips a week from Detroit to Put-in-Bay. With a capacity of 3,500 passengers, her dance floor was 200 feet long. On Labor Day, islanders gathered at the dock to bid her farewell until the following year as the band played "Auld Lang Syne."

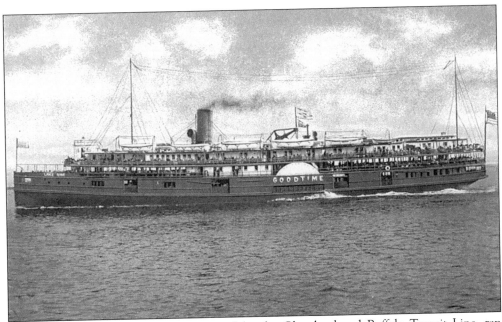

From 1925 to 1938, the *Goodtime*, owned by the Cleveland and Buffalo Transit Line, ran regularly from Cleveland to Cedar Point and Put-in-Bay. Large steamers eventually ceased operation, partly because federal legislation designed for ocean liners made demands on lake boats that were too expensive to meet for a three-month season.

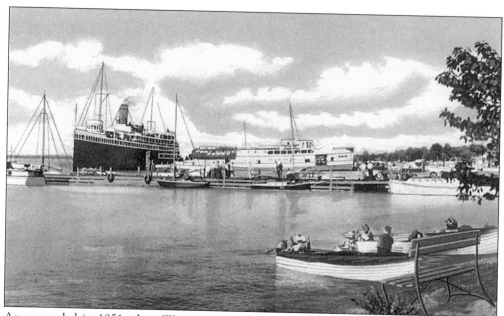

An era ended in 1951 when *Western States* was the last of the grand old steamers to make regularly scheduled trips to Put-in-Bay. Since then, it has been ferries that bring passengers to the islands. The *Mystic Isle* ferry is pictured here at the far side of the dock.

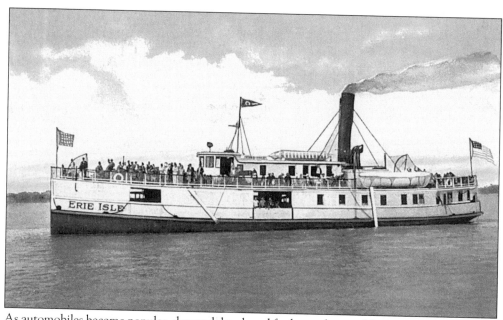

As automobiles became popular, demand developed for boats that could transport cars as well as people to the islands. The first ferries were boats towing scows or barges carrying cars. The *Erie Isle* was the first to carry cars and people on the same vessel. Beginning in the early 1930s, she ran from Catawba to Put-in-Bay with a capacity of 300 passengers and 13 cars.

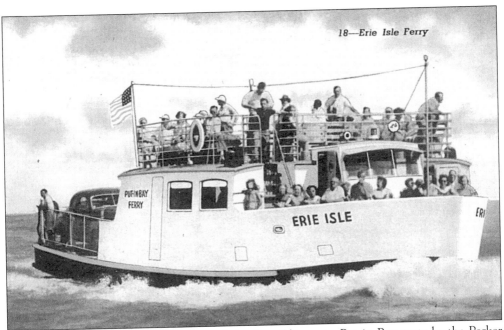

In 1952, the second *Erie Isle* was assigned the Port Clinton to Put-in-Bay route by the Parker Boat Line. At 61 feet in length, the vessel was more economical to operate and could make more frequent trips than its predecessors.

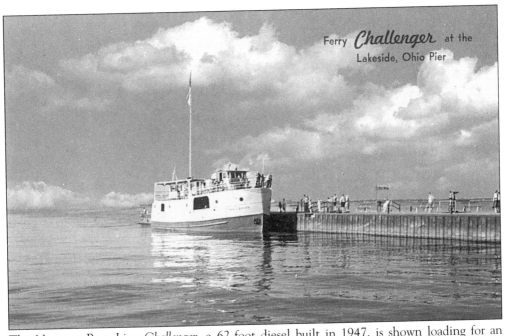

The Neuman Boat Line *Challenger*, a 62-foot diesel built in 1947, is shown loading for an excursion at the Lakeside dock. The Neuman Boat Line has been in operation since 1907. For some years in the 1940s, Neuman boats ran from Sandusky to Put-in-Bay, but shifted in the 1950s to the Marblehead to Kellys Island route.

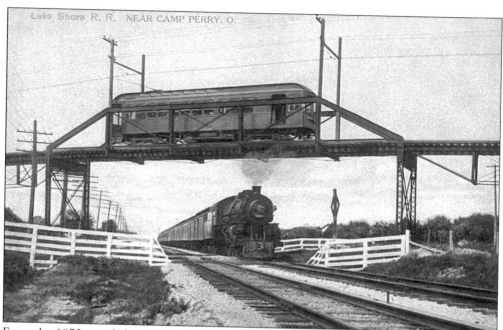

From the 1870s until the 1920s, the Lake Shore and Michigan Southern Railroad ran from Toledo to Cleveland with stops at Camp Perry, Port Clinton, Gypsum, and Danbury. Near Camp Perry, a trestle permitted the interurban to cross over the railroad tracks. The Lake Shore and Michigan Southern became the New York Central in the 1920s.

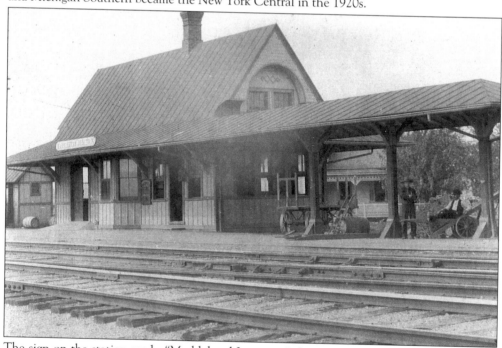

The sign on the station reads, "Marblehead Junction," the name used by the Lake Shore and Southern Railroad from 1886 to 1904. The name, confusing because of a several-mile separation from Marblehead, was eventually changed to Danbury. The station was also used by the Lakeside and Marblehead Railroad.

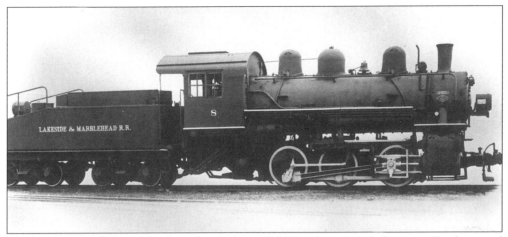

The Lakeside and Marblehead Railroad claimed 6.88 miles of track between Danbury and Marblehead. Freight service operated from 1887 to 1964, primarily to haul limestone from the quarry. At Danbury, cars were switched to the Lake Shore and later to the New York Central, and moving 100 cars a day was average during busy years. Engine Number 8, pictured here, served the area during the 1940s.

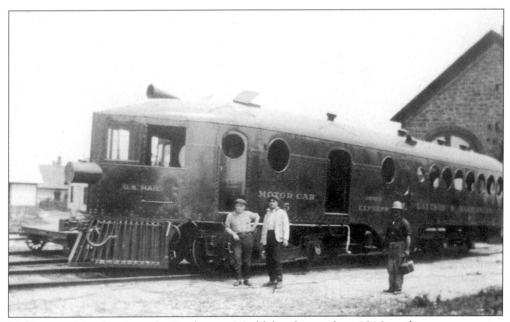

McKeen car Number 5 ran the Danbury to Marblehead route from 1916 until passenger service ended in 1930. Painted red and powered by a six-cylinder gasoline motor, the car was affectionately known as the "Red Devil." Jay Owens, leaning on the car, was the motorman, and George Wiedenholt, beside him, was conductor. The third man is unidentified.

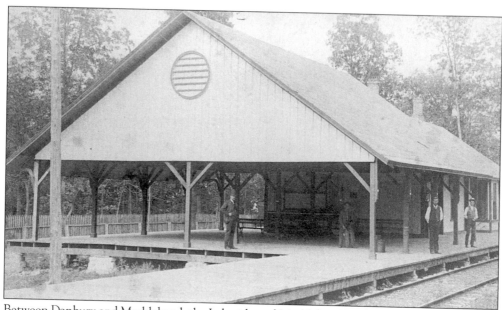

Between Danbury and Marblehead, the Lakeside and Marblehead Railroad made stops at Picolo and Violet. It also stopped at the Lakeside station, located near Seventh Street and Cedar Avenue beside the Lakeside campground. The open end of the station was closed some years after passenger service was terminated.

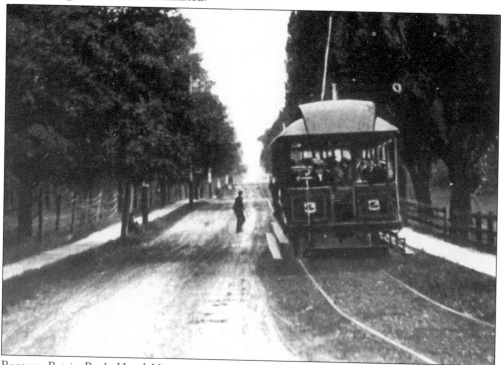

Because Put-in-Bay's Hotel Victory was a mile and a half from the steamboat landing, an electric trolley line was built to accommodate hotel guests. Built c.1892, the line ceased operation soon after the hotel fire of 1919. Here, a trolley car with a capacity of 96 passengers is pictured on Catawba Avenue.

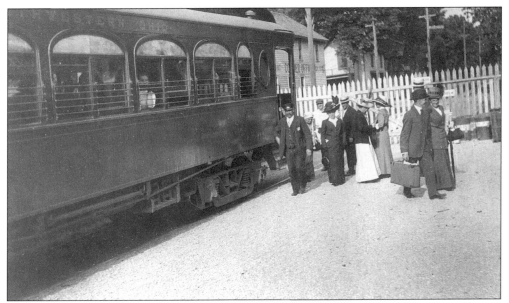

From 1905 to 1939, an electric railway or trolley ran from Toledo to Marblehead via Elmore, Oak Harbor, Port Clinton, and Lakeside. Originally incorporated as the Toledo, Port Clinton, and Lakeside Railway, it was eventually owned by the Ohio Public Service Company. The Lakeside station consisted of a roof on posts at Fifth Street and Walnut Avenue, where passengers are shown arriving.

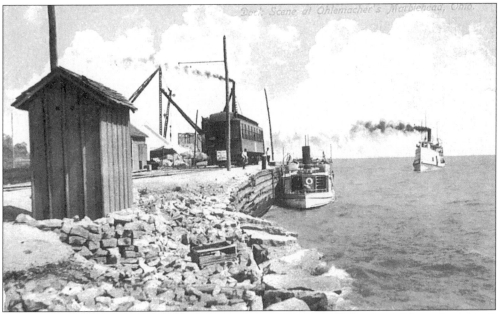

From 1908 to 1911, the interurban ran through downtown Marblehead to Ohlemacher's Dock at the point of the peninsula. Passengers could transfer to the *Hazel* to cross the bay to downtown Sandusky. From 1922 to 1926, the interurban ran to the end of Bay Point for an even shorter boat ride to Sandusky.

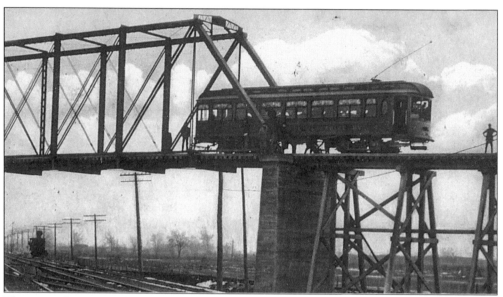

The interurban entered Port Clinton from the west by crossing Fremont Road, then traveled through town on Fourth Street. Here, a car traverses a trestle on the east end of town that crossed the railroad tracks near State Street.

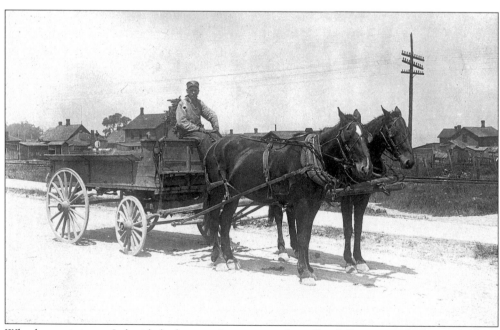

Whether arriving at Lakeside by boat, train, or interurban, Frank Sauvey might be available to haul baggage to your cottage, rooming house, or hotel.

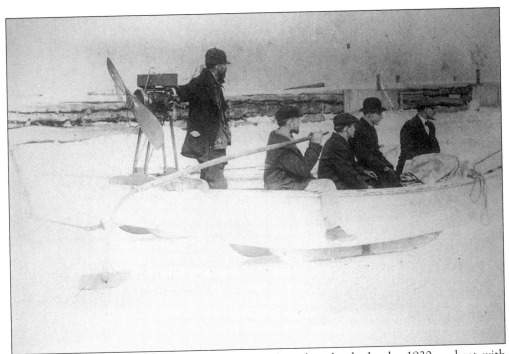

During winter months, contractors delivered mail to the islands. In the 1920s, a boat with runners was used, as a mounted engine could propel the boat over the ice. Oars were on board for use in open water. The group on board in this photograph includes William "Bad Axe" Smith, Harry Rice, Fritz Critz, unknown, and Dan McKenzie.

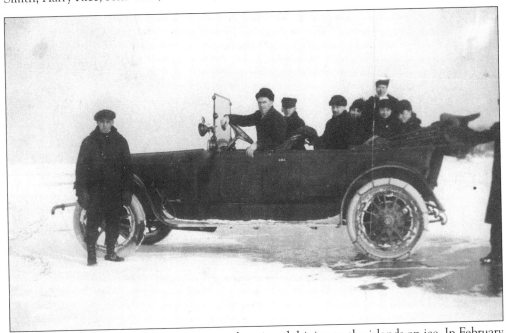

When automobiles entered the scene, people enjoyed driving to the islands on ice. In February 1918, John, Dan, and Ralph Carroll, along with their friends, were the first to drive from Lakeside to Kellys Island.

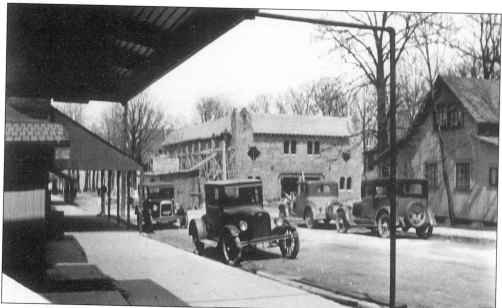

Automobiles began to appear around 1900, and were quite common by the 1920s. These cars were parked on Walnut Avenue in Lakeside during the winter of 1927-1928, when Orchestra Hall was under construction. A ferry brought autos from Sandusky to a peninsula landing near the location of Dempsey Access.

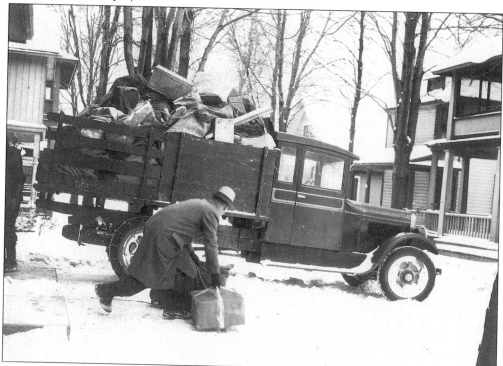

When the Lakeside Association purchased its first truck, maintenance workers were relieved of caring for horses. This truck is shown being loaded with trash on a day when snow covers the ground.

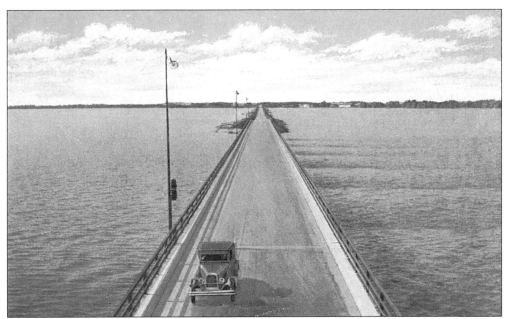

The 1929 opening of the two-lane Sandusky Bay Bridge allowed passengers to bypass Fremont on the trip from Sandusky to Port Clinton. This bridge, just over two miles long, was replaced by the four-lane Edison Bridge in the 1970s. Its center was removed, and the approaches are now used as fishing piers.

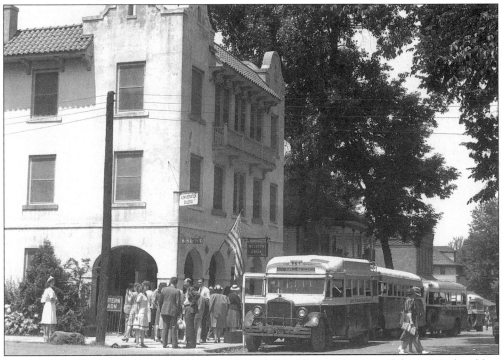

During to the Depression of the 1930s, and World War II gas rationing of the 1940s, local bus lines served the area and connected with larger carriers at Port Clinton or Sandusky. In the 1940s, special busses were arranged for conference delegates at Lakeside.

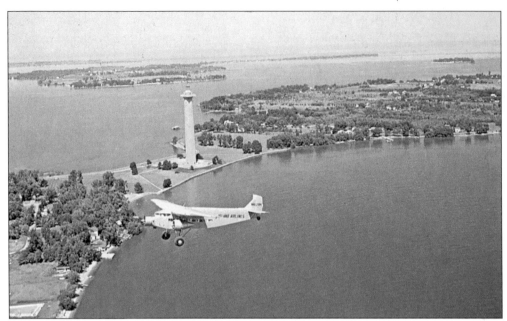

In 1930, Erie Isle Airways, later known as Island Airlines, began flights to the islands. The maximum flight of "the shortest airline in the world" is approximately six miles from the airfield near Port Clinton to Put-in-Bay. Original biplanes with open cockpits were replaced by the Ford tri-motor "tin goose," which offered a metal body as an alternative to the wood and cloth of many other planes.

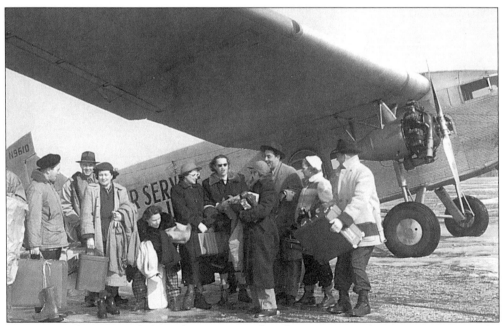

Having an airline meant daily mail service, as well as the opportunity for a priest to come to the island regularly for Mass, or for islanders to reach the mainland for medical emergencies. Air travel also ushered in a new era for winter tourism.